The Friendly Floppy
Ragdoll Cat

Kimberly H. Maxwell

New Chapter Publishing, LLC
Mountain Home, North Carolina

Cover and interior design by Kimberly H. Maxwell

Photo Credits
Front cover photo is Tessie from Fur Real Ragdolls in CA. She is a pet quality seal point mitted Ragdoll. The photo was taken by her owner Marsha Harris. Tessie's half brother Quincy is also in the book.

Interior images were taken by the cat's owner, or the author, unless otherwise noted with photo. See the list of contributors in the back of the book.

Back cover photos: Top photo is Kylador's Basil, a blue bicolor, owner and breeder is Karen Wright in Canada. Middle photo is PalaceCats Armani, a seal mitted kitten by breeder Shalane Doucette in Florida. Bottom photo is Alissa Pendorf's blue lynx bicolor, Jazzmania Raina doing the "Ragdoll-flop."

Edition ISBN's: See TheFriendlyFloppyRagdollCat.com for more information
    978-0-9839860-2-7 Published 2012 Hardcover
    978-0-9839860-7-2 Published 2014 Paperback Abrdiged Edition

ISBN-13: 978-0-9839860-7-2

Publisher's Cataloging-in-Publication Data

    Pets / Cats / Breeds / Ragdoll
    Pets / Cats / Care / Health
    Pets / Cats / General
    Animal Culture / Pets / Cats / Ragdoll
    Veterinary Medicine / General

Published by
New Chapter Publishing, LLC
PO Box 844
Mountain Home, NC 28758

Printed in the United States of America

To my family, friends, and felines, who have touched my life, and heart— especially my husband for his unwavering support, my cousin Dr. Shaylene Snyder, DVM for her knowledgeable input, and to my parents for instilling the belief that I can do whatever I set my mind to. Lastly, to the cat owners and breeders, who contributed their photos and time to help me reach my goal, and to those of you who purchased this book.

Contents

I adore the Ragdoll breed, but I may not be the author you would expect. I am not a breeder, and have never written a book. I do not own purebred Ragdolls, and had not even heard of them until 1999. This book would have been completed earlier if I had not had help from my Ragdoll "wannabe's" Mr. Tyler and Ms. Trinity. It seems they thought I should take ample breaks to pet and play with them.

After losing my dad, grandma, and my first cat, Skeamer, I finally got my priorities in order and closed my retail store, that required so much of my time. In December of 2008, I had the idea to compose a book mainly of photos and quotations. That thought evolved in to this book. I have learned so much owning cats, starting in 1990. I wanted to share my findings with fellow cat lovers and simply talk all-things-cat, specifically one of my favorite breeds, the Ragdoll. I find it hard to fathom that with all the Ragdoll books I have bought, only a few went into specifics about the breed. I especially wanted to see more pictures showing the different colors and patterns. That desire is what motivated me to write this book.

The hundreds of photos in these pages were taken by their cat owners, unless otherwise specified, who were kind enough to grant me permission to use them. I would have enjoyed meeting all the lovable cats, their owners and breeders in person. I am grateful to Denny and Laura Dayton for returning my email and phone correspondence. Both were so gracious of their time, especially not knowing me and having been retired many years from breeding Ragdolls. With the role they played in getting the Ragdoll officially recognized, I would have been honored to meet them in person.

Having pets is a commitment for the life of your pet. My cats are my children, and are a part of our family. Vacations and travel would be easier, and not having vet bills or an occasional pet crisis would be nice, but to me the joy definitely outweighs the not-so-good. Some day I may actually get my purebred Ragdolls, but for now I am perfectly happy enjoying each day, just the way it is.

Kim H Maxwell

Have you ever heard of a floppy cat?

The International Cat Association states the Ragdoll is one of the fastest growing breeds, second only to the Bengal. According to the Cat Fancier's Association, the Ragdoll is the fourth most popular breed.

If you've never heard of a Ragdoll cat or already own one, and would like to learn more about this wonderful breed of cat— this book is for you.

Learn about the Ragdoll-flop. Read about everything from the Ragdoll beginning, to "saying goodbye." Discover the Ragdoll colors and patterns with hundreds of full color photos.

This book covers Ragdoll characteristics, traits, history, breed standard, bringing your kitten home to caring for your elderly cat, grooming care, food, litter and litter boxes, deterring unwanted behavior, travel, dangers, emergencies, disease, health, vaccinations, tips for finding a veterinarian and choosing a breeder. Also included is a list of questions to ask before you adopt, plus extensive resources, references and links.

We know the breed to be a large, floppy, dog-like, cuddly cat. The Ragdoll is known for its affectionate personality. Most Raggies are great with people and other pets. They are trusting enough to flop belly-up for a tummy rub. They are outgoing and playful but not hyper or lazy.

It is not hard to choose the friendly Ragdoll as a wonderful breed of cat, but it is hard to choose which color and pattern with all the beautiful choices!

Karen Wilkinson's
Gizmo, a cream bicolor

The Remarkable Ragdoll

Ragdolls are known for their soft coat, large size, striking blue eyes and pleasant temperament. They were given their breed name because of the way some go limp when you pick them up, like a rag doll. If you spend time talking with Ragdoll owners it won't be long before you hear about the "Ragdoll-flop." Most Ragdolls will lie on their back, belly exposed, as relaxed as can be.

Many owners say their Ragdoll is the ultimate puppy-cat. They are typically good for families, and usually accepting of children and dogs. Some Ragdoll owners even say their Ragdoll is good with birds, rabbits or guinea pigs. I would only allow short supervised visits until I was positive my Ragdoll was compatible with other animals or children.

The Ragdoll breed is a fine woven tapestry with the best features of several breeds. Ragdolls have the laid-back personality of the Persian without the demanding grooming needs, the intense blue eyes of the Siamese, and the large size of the beautiful Maine Coon.

Karen Wilkinson's Fred (cream bicolor) doing the Ragdoll-flop

Sandy Baker's Rocky (seal lynx mitted) and Pippin (seal mitted) with Duncan the Quaker Parrot

CH AngelPersians Snowbelle of Beauty Purrs Cattery, a copper eyed white Persian

Blumoon O' Kentucky's Heartsong-n-Joy, a blue point Siamese

Nyree Glapp's Meddle, a black silver tabby blotched Maine Coon

*R*agdolls want to play and interact with their people and follow you around the house. They know just how to "help" you exercise, work in the office, in the bathroom, on the stairs, in the kitchen and with the laundry.

Kylador's Bridlepath Mercedes with kitten

Kylador's Canadian Chloe with kittens

Karen Wilkinson's Fred

Constance McCarthy's Nicodemus

Macair Skelton-Angeles (blue bicolor A-typical) RockStarDolls Sir Augustine "Auggie"

Kylador Watson

Kylador As You Like It "Basil"

They are not usually climbers and tend to stay on the floor— but are not lazy cats. Some Ragdolls can even be clicker-trained and have been known to learn to walk on a leash or play fetch.

Ragdolls are not overly vocal but will carry on their own little conversation with chirps, meeps, trills and meows.

Contrary to false early claims, they are not impervious to pain, and even though they are docile, when threatened most will defend themselves and react like all other cats. Ragdolls tend to be trusting, easy going and should be kept inside.

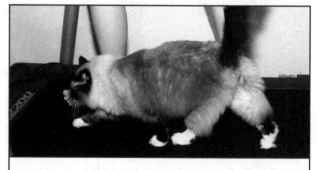

Sandy Baker's Pippin sharing the treadmill

Kylador Kitten

Kylador As You Like It "Basil"

DollHeaven Lexus of Kylador "Lexie"

Kylador Watson

Sandy Baker's Rocky

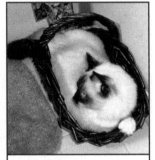

Sandy Baker's Pippin

Sandy Baker's Pippin

Sandy Baker's Pippin

Kylador Watson

Mary Becker's Tedrick "Teddy"

Kylador Kitten

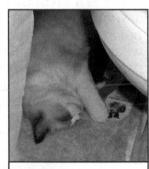

Kylador Kitten

Krista Tulle's Kylador Zeus

Linda Dicmanis Schniffley

Gloie Wall's Katie

Gloie Wall's Benji

Mary Becker's Toulouse "Touie"
(blue point mitted)

Gail Vettel of Angel Kissed Ragdolls
(blue mitted colorpoint) kitten

There is a myth that Ragdolls do not shed and are hypoallergenic. These claims are not completely accurate. Cat hair is not what causes the allergen, it is the Fel d 1 protein found in the saliva that creates the dander, and Ragdolls have this too. For a medium-to-long-haired cat, the Ragdoll's bunny-like, plush coat does mat and shed less than some other breeds because they have more long guard hairs, and less undercoat, or secondary down hair.

The internet, cat shows, and online groups are great places to learn about the breed. I am in several Yahoo! Ragdoll groups and I've met some wonderful people. Most of the pictures in this book are from the people I have met in those groups.

Bridlepath Mercedes "Sadie"
(seal bicolor) belonging to
Karen Wright of Kylador Cattery

*Y*ou will not find any extreme features on a Ragdoll, other than its extremely great personality.

Common standards in appearance are for

- a large cat with medium to large bone structure, firm and muscular, no fat except for a moderate fat pad on the greater omentum or lower abdomen

- sturdy, medium to long size leg length, large hind quarters that are slightly higher than the front legs, with large round and tufted paws

- broad chest, short neck, and heavy set, with a longer coat around the neck (ruff) framing the face

- proportional large head shape should be a modified wedge, full cheeks with a rounded muzzle, and a well developed full chin

- gently curved profile with a straight last segment to the nose, without a nose break

- flat plane between ears with rounded medium sized ears that tilt slightly forward and are wide at the base

- large oval or almond shaped vivid blue eyes (deep dark blue preferred) that are slightly slanted with outer corners level with the base of the ear

- medium-to-long hair that lays close to the body without a thick undercoat; coat is silky and dense, breaking as the cat moves

- long bushy plumed tail that is slightly tapered

Alissa Pendorf's Raina (blue lynx bicolor)

Karen Wilkinson's Myst (blue colorpoint)

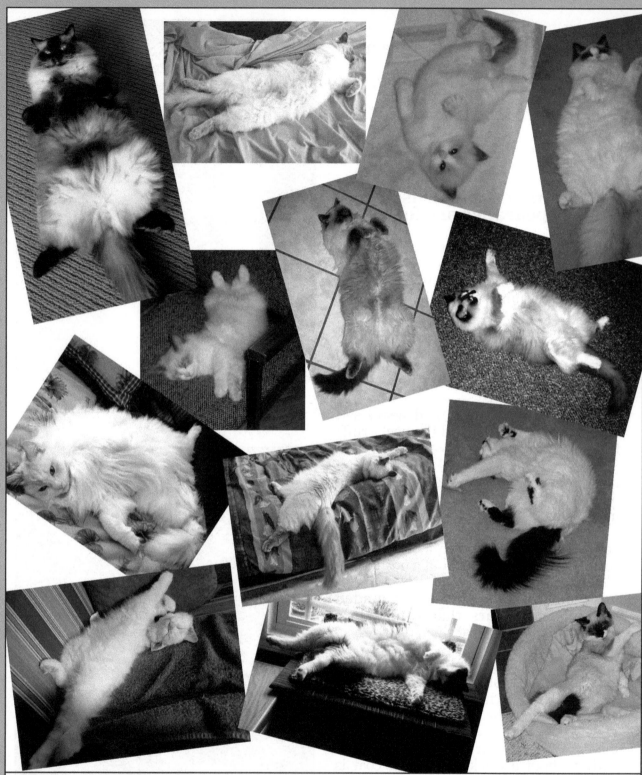

Row One Constance McCarthy's Nicodemus. Linda Dicmanis' Bingo. Karen Wright's of Kylador's kitten, then Iris
Row Two Karen Wright of Kylador's kitten. Cindy Forst's Lili. Lynn Jasper's Bella
Row Three Marsha Harris' Quincy. Linda Dicmanis' Bingo. Kimberly Maxwell's Trinity
Row Four Gloie Wall's Benji. Kimberly Maxwell's Tyler. Sonja Phillips' Brody

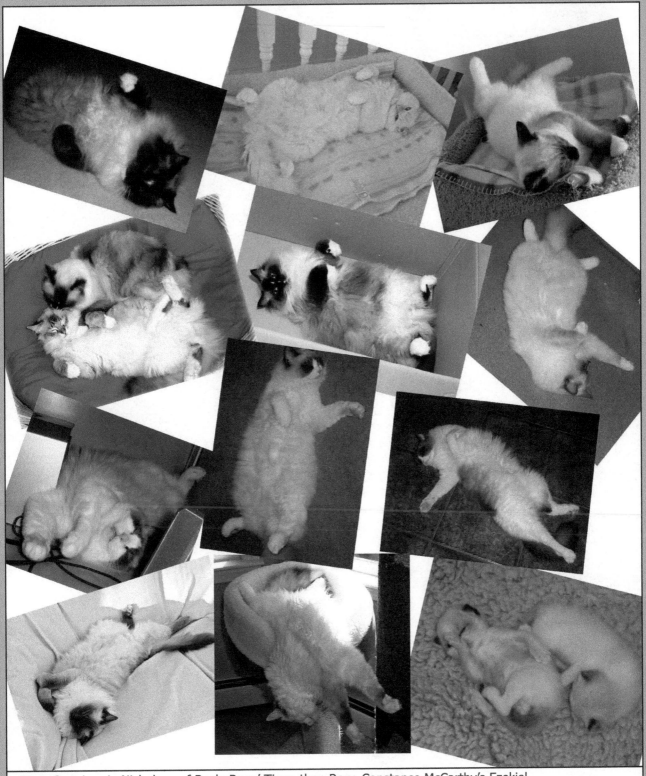

Row One Laurie Nicholson of RocknRagz' Tiger, then Rory. Constance McCarthy's Ezekiel
Row Two Sandra Baker's Rocky and Pippin, then Pippin. Karen Wright of Kylador's Paddy
Row Three Karen Wright of Kylador's Watson, then Chloe, the and Basil
Row Four Karen Wilkinson's Myst. Sandra Baker's Rocky. Karen Wright of Kylador's kittens

Sonja Phillip's Tucker (seal point mitted) and brother Cody (blue colorpoint) Leap year babies

Colors and Patterns

Ragdolls do not fully mature, reaching full color until around two years old, and full size and weight, until they are three to four years old. All pointed Ragdolls are born nearly pure white. While in the womb the kittens are warm, but within a few days after they are birthed you will start to see the colors darken where their body temperature is typically lower. Colors darken first on the cats' extremities or points (legs, feet, face, head, ears, and tail). It is also believed that Ragdolls that live in areas or homes with cooler temperatures become darker than those kept in warmer climates.

In some of the Ragdoll groups I belong to, discussions often come up about solids or mink Ragdolls, in colors such as black, white, smoke, silver, sepia, cinnamon or fawn with eye color other than blue. Unlike pointed Ragdolls, mink and sepia colors can be born with a lighter color of their darker adult color, and they typically get much darker as adults. The minks usually have an aqua or blue-green eye color. A discussion about the RagaMuffin breed usually follows.

According to the breed standard for Ragdolls there are four patterns: colorpoint, mitted, bicolor, and van. A colorpoint cat has darker extremities or points with a lighter body color. In Ragdolls the points may be solid, lynx, tortie, or torbie. The points are partially overlaid with white in the mitted, bicolor and van pattens.

The patterns come in six colors: seal and the dilute chocolate, blue and the dilute lilac that some call frost, red that some call flame, and the dilute cream.

Laurie Nicholson of RocknRagz
eight week old blue point mitted kitten

Karen Wright of Kylador's seal bicolor kitten

Karen Wilkinson's Merlin (seal point mitted) and Myst (blue colorpoint)

Watching the colors come in

Row One Nancie East's O'Malley, a chocolate mitted lynx and Reilly, a mitted torbie. Alissa Pendorf's Raina,
Row Two My wannabe's Tyler, a seal bicolor and Trinity, a seal bicolor van. Debbie LeStrange of GuysnDolls Crux,
Row Three Constance McCarthy's Ezekiel, a seal mitted and Nicodemus, a seal colorpoint. Karen Wilkinson's Shalane Doucette of PalaceCats Maximus, a blue bicolor.
Row Four Marsha Harris' Quincy, a flame bicolor, then Tessie, a seal mitted. Gloie Wall's Benji, a flame mitted lynx,
Row Five Laurie Nicholson's of RocknRagz Bindi Lou, a seal mitted tortie, then Charming Chico, a lilac Snuggler, a chocolate torbie bicolor. Caroline Parris' (wannabe) Angel, a seal colorpoint.

as the cats mature

a blue bicolor lynx. Linda Dicmanis Shniffley, a seal colorpoint, then Bingo, a blue colorpoint.
a chocolate bicolor then Casper, a lilac bicolor. Sonja Phillip's Cody, a blue colorpoint and Tucker, a seal color point.
Fred, a cream bicolor. Mary Becker's Teddy, a seal mitted lynx and Touie, a blue point mitted with a blaze.

then Katie, a seal colorpoint. Sandra Baker's Pippin, a seal colorpoint with a blaze, then Rocky, a seal mitted lynx.
colorpoint, then Royal William, a cream colorpoint, then PalaceDolls Abby Rose, a blue bicolor. Eve Kurpier's

Constance McCarthy's Nicodemus (seal colorpoint)	Rags2Riches Elijah of PalaceCats (blue point mitted)	Marsha Harris' Quincy (flame bicolor)

Seal points are a deep brown to almost black. Body color is between light brown or beige/ivory. The seal colors will have deep brown nose leather and paw pads.

Blue points are a cool slate gray color on the points. Body is a light gray or bluish white/beige. Their nose leather and paw pads will be a slate blue gray color.

Red points also called flame points, are a deep reddish orange to bright apricot, the darker and hotter points are preferred. Body is a warm creamy white. Nose leather will be coral pink to flesh color. The red gene is found in reds or flames, creams, tortie and torbie.

Color is determined by a cats genes and alleles. Genetic factors also decide how dense or dilute the color is. Some like the red gene are a sex-linked color. DNA testing can be used to determine color.

Debbie Le-Strange of GuysnDolls Lumiere (chocolate point lynx)	Mary Ewen of Drouindolls' Angelica (lilac point lynx)	Karen Wilkinson's Gizmo (cream bicolor)

Chocolate points are a warm milk chocolate color. Body is light beige/ivory. Their nose leather and paw pads are almost a burnt rose to cinnamon, salmon pink color— lighter than a seal brown.

Lilac or frost points are a frosty light gray/beige with a slight pink cast. Body is a light ivory/white. Nose leather and paw pads are a pinkish lavender color.

Cream points are a soft apricot or buff to light pinkish cream color— not a hot color. Body is a creamy white. Paw pads and nose leather are a rosy pink.

The colors seal and blue seem to be the easiest to find. The ear color is the deciding factor in determining the point color, or a DNA test which is more accurate.

Both top photos are Linda Dicmanis Ragdolls, Bingo shown twice (blue colorpoint) and Schniffley (seal colorpoint)

Colorpoint Ragdolls have the classic pointed markings with no white anywhere in their coat. Their point color is darkest on their ears, mask or face, not extending over the top of the head, tail and legs, including the feet. These points should be darker than the body, with well defined color and a definite difference between the darker point color on the extremities and the lighter body color. The chest, bib and chin can be lighter than the points. They may be solid, lynx, tortie or torbie. The nose leather and paw pads should be fully pigmented and match the point color. Ragdolls are not the only pointed cats. You will also find the pointed pattern in breeds like the Siamese, Balinese, Himalayan and Birman.

The **mitted** pattern is just like the pointed, but with symmetrical white mittens on the feet. The white mitts should go up to and around the wrist joint in the front. The back feet should have white boots that go all the way up and around the hock, no higher than mid thigh. The chin must be white extending in to the belly stripe, varying in width from the bib between the front legs to the underside. Like the non-mitted colorpoint, their nose leather should be fully pigmented and match the point color. The mitted colorpoint may have a white blaze in the shape of a diamond, line, star, or hourglass central on their face. It can be broken, or a symmetrical patch of white anywhere from their nose leather up to their forehead.

Karen Wright of Kylador's Samo Sue
(seal point mitted)

Mary Ewen of Drouindolls' Madison
(seal mitted with a blaze)

Bicolors should have a white inverted, symmetrical "V" on their face that remains within the outer edges of their eyes. The chin, chest, and underbody should be white, as well as the feet and legs, with only minor dark spots allowed. The point color is restricted to the ears, tail and outer parts of the mask. It should be dense and clearly defined with only minor white spotting. The saddle area can be a lighter shade of the point color and may show white spotting. Their nose leather should be pink as well as the paw pads but a mixture of color on the paw pads and fur is acceptable because of the two colors in the pattern.

Lynn Freeman's Nolte (blue bicolor)

The **van** pattern is also called high white. Point color is restricted to the ears, tail and mask and should be dense and well defined, with only minor white spotting. The point color on the mask may be limited to the upper part of the head, and show gradual fading of color. The majority of the body is white, as are the legs and feet with only minor spotting. The nose leather and paw pads should be pink. I found breeders specifically breeding for this pattern, the hardest to find. Apparently it is a hard pattern to achieve the show quality breed standard.

Kristi Pemberton's HeatherHill Birmingham Al of BigCityDolls "Albert" (blue van bicolor)

All **torties** are unique, with a one-of-a-kind pattern. The tortie is a multi-color mottled effect, sort of like a tortoiseshell or calico with patches and splashes of color that are darker on the points. In Ragdolls, a tortie comes in colors, blue, seal, chocolate and lilac. A tortie will still be called a color such as a seal tortie or blue tortie depending on the coloring. Some call a blue tortie a blue cream. Cream is the dilute of red, which is also called flame. There is not a flame tortie, red tortie or cream tortie because the red or dilute of it, with the other color,

PalaceCats Denim n Lace (blue cream tortie)

Laurie Nicholson of RocknRagz Bindi Lou (seal tortie mitted)

Sandra Baker's Rocky
(seal lynx mitted)

Eve Kurpiers' Snuggler
(chocolate torbie bicolor)

Lynn Jasper's Isabella "Bella"
(seal point mitted)

is what makes them a tortie. Torties are almost always female cats due to the sex-linked red gene or X chromosome. In the rare instance that a tortie is male, it is usually sterile or may need to be older before becoming fertile.

Some call the **lynx** pattern, a tabby pattern. The lynx pattern gives a striped effect on the face, legs and tail. They also have a thin line of white around their eyes and on the inside of their ears at the outside edge, like liner. Lynx Ragdolls have

PalaceCats Sylvester
(blue point lynx)

an "M" marking on their foreheads and reddish nose leather. Lynx tend to appear a lighter shade than a non-lynx of the same color. The striped pattern shows up the most in the darker colors. The lynx pattern can be found in colorpoint, mitted and bicolor. The lynx striping, which is also called barring, is caused by the agouti gene. Some non-lynx kittens will look like they have striped markings, but unless it is a lynx these stripes are called ghost barring and fade with age. The ghost barring seems to show up more on flames and creams.

A **torbie** is a mix of a tortie plus lynx. Both torties and torbies are available in colorpoint, mitted and bicolor.

If you are looking for a Ragdoll and don't plan to show, a "mismark" is a wonderful way to get a full bred Ragdoll. A mismark simply means that the Ragdoll is not marked correctly for showing. They are sold as pet quality, but other than their outward appearance, the temperament, size and characteristics should be the same as a perfectly marked show quality Ragdoll.

Shalane Doucette's RW SGC BoysnRags Maximus "Max" of PalaceCats (blue bicolor)

There are many **cat registries**. Each registry has its own set of breed standards and colors it will accept. Below is a partial list of the main registries. See the "Resources and Reference" section in the back of the book for an in-depth listing.

- ACA American Cat Association (USA)

- AACE American Association of Cat Enthusiast (USA) aaceinc.org

- ACFA American Cat Fanciers' Association (USA) acfacat.com

- CCA Canadian Cat Association cca-afc.com/en

- CFA Cat Fanciers' Association (USA) cfa.org

- CFF Cat Fanciers' Federation (USA) cffinc.org

- FiFe Federation International Feline fifeweb.org

- GCCF Governing Council of the Cat Fancy (UK) gccfcats.org

- TICA The International Cat Association tica.org

There are different classes that cats can be shown. TICA has Championship Breeds, Non-Championship Breeds, like Household Pet and Household Pet Kitten, Advanced New Breeds and Preliminary New Breeds. TICA recognizes Ragdolls in the Championship Breed. At this time the RagaMuffin can only be registered with TICA.

CFA recognizes the following competition Classes: Kitten, Championship, Premiership, Provisional, Miscellaneous, Veteran and Household Pet. The CFA registered Ragdolls in 1993. They accepted bicolor and van Ragdolls for Championship in 2000 and in 2008 accepted Ragdolls in mitted and colorpoint also. The CFA says Ragdolls are a large, blue-eyed cat, with a laid-back personality.

Altered males weigh between 10 to 20 pounds and females range between 10 to 15 pounds at maturity.

According to Ragdolls of America Group (RAG) at ragdollscfa.org the CFA breed standard for Ragdolls was modified in 2009. See cfainc.org/breeds/standards/ragdoll.pdf for more information.

Nancy East's O'Malley (chocolate lynx mitted)

Jenny Moylan's Shiloh (flame bicolor)

The RagaMuffin was accepted into the Miscellaneous Class by CFA in February 2003. Then in 2009 they accepted RagaMuffins for Provisional status in the longhair division and to Championship Class in February, 2011. They do not accept the pointed pattern.

The breed standard for some breeds like the Ragdoll, RagaMuffin, and Maine Coon actually include a temperament or disposition standard in addition to physical standards. TICA calls for Ragdoll temperament to be unchallenging.

Trexdolls Fergie of RockstarDolls "Fergie" (seal tortie point)

Tara Rerrie's Dixter,
a red mackerel tabby RagaMuffin

Barbara Müller-Walter's Maxwell Smart,
a black silver classic tabby Maine Coon

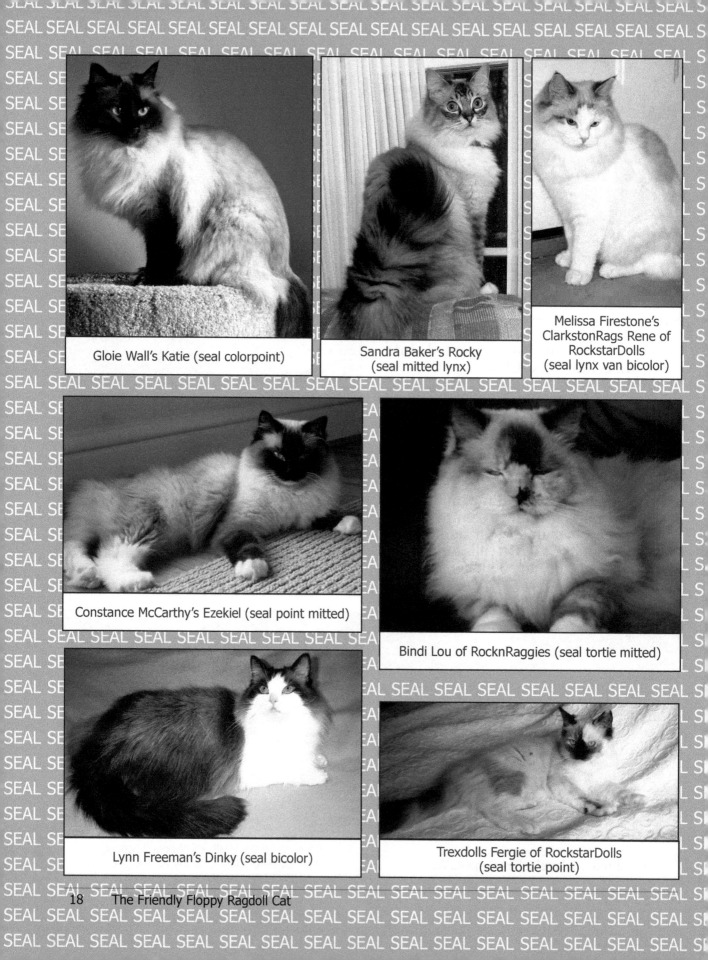

Gloie Wall's Katie (seal colorpoint)

Sandra Baker's Rocky
(seal mitted lynx)

Melissa Firestone's
ClarkstonRags Rene of
RockstarDolls
(seal lynx van bicolor)

Constance McCarthy's Ezekiel (seal point mitted)

Bindi Lou of RocknRaggies (seal tortie mitted)

Lynn Freeman's Dinky (seal bicolor)

Trexdolls Fergie of RockstarDolls
(seal tortie point)

Debbie Le-Strange of GuysnDolls
Neytiri (chocolate bicolor)

Debbie Le-Strange of GuysnDolls
Diana (chocolate point lynx)

Nancie East's O'Malley
(chocolate lynx mitted)

Eve Kurpiers' Snuggler
(chocolate torbie bicolor)

Debbie Le-Strange's GuysnDolls Amberglade
Chocolat Delite "Neo" (chocolate colorpoint)

Alissa Pendorf's Raina (blue lynx bicolor)

Shalane Doucette's RW SGC BoysnrRags Maximus "Max" of PalaceCats (blue bicolor)

Kristi Pemberton's HeatherHill Birmingham Al "Albert" of BigCityDolls (blue van bicolor)

Mary Becker's Toulouse "Touie" (blue point mitted with small blaze)

NenesRags Rujam Molly of PalaceCats (blue cream torbie)

Debbie Le-Strange's GuysnDolls Kiwimagic New Zealand Pride "Pascal" (blue colorpoint)

Trexdolls Phoebe of RockstarDolls (blue tortie point bicolor)

Mrs. Mary Owen of DrouinDolls'
Angelica (lilac lynx point)

Mrs. Mary Owen of DrouinDolls'
Summer (lilac bicolor)

Laurie Nicholson's LionsRoyale Charming Chico
of RocknRagz (lilac colorpoint)

Nancie East's Murphey
(flame colorpoint)

Gloie Wall's Benji
(flame point mitted lynx)

Melissa Firestone of RockstarDolls
flame mitted kitten

Jenny Moylan's Shiloh (flame bicolor)

Karen Wilkinson's Gizmo and Fred
(both cream bicolors)

Pia Venbrant's Bozidara's Diego 4 Hvenhildas
"Diego" (cream point mitted)

Laurie Nicholson's Royale William of RocknRagz
(cream colorpoint)

White, Black, Smoke, Silver, Cinnamon, Fawn,

Angela Kostellansky of Three Rivers Ragdolls'
RockstarDolls Sterling Brooke (blue mink mitted)

Suzanne Leonhard of Hollywood Ragdolls'
RockstarDolls Lady Arabella Blue (blue mink mitted)

Pia Venbrant's Hvenhildas Creame Brylé
(blue classic torbie mitted)

Pia Venbrant's Sundari's Kali of Hvenhildas "Kali"
(black bicolor)

Rovena E. Parmley's
Tuftytoes Rubin (blue white/mitted)

Kiristi Pemberton's Bakerspaws Miss Lacey
Washington "Lacey" of BigCityDolls
(lilac point mink bicolor)

Sepia, Mink ...

Patricia Besaw's Bellapalazzo Sir Bentley
(BEW, blue-eyed white)

The cats represented on these two pages are registered as Ragdolls in the various cat registries in the US, Belgium, and Sweden— mostly with TICA.

White is a dominant gene that masks the actual color of a cat. White Ragdolls may look "solid" but are actually blue-eyed pointed cats with the true point color masked by white. The color can be identified with a DNA test.

According to Melissa Firestone of Rockstar Ragdolls "sepias can only be created mating a mink to a mink."

Melissa Firestone's of RockstarDolls Mink Jagger
(seal mitted mink)

Kristi Pemberton's RockstarDolls Kokomo Sepia
Starlet of BigCityDolls (seal sepia mitted)

Mary Susan McAuliff of Windy-Gable's RockstarDolls
KC of WindyGables (blue mink) RockstarDolls Music
To My Ears of WindyGables (seal mink mitted)
photo by Barbara Link-Poulson

Melissa Firestone's RustsRagdolls Mabel Mink
Bluebell "Mabel" of RockstarDolls (blue mink mitted)

Tara Rerrie's Dixter,
a red mackerel tabby RagaMuffin

Ragdoll or RagaMuffin
What's the difference?

Ragdolls and RagaMuffins originated from the original Ann Baker, International Ragdoll Cat Association (IRCA) lines. RagaMuffins are accepted by the various cat fancy registries in more colors than the Ragdoll, and are allowed eye color other than blue, including odd-eyed where the eyes are each a different color.

The RagaMuffin breed standard calls for a medium to long coat of thick, dense silky hair and is allowed in all colors and patterns, including tortoiseshell, solids and mink. CFA states "every color and pattern is allowable with or without white, except pointed colors."

*T*he RagaMuffin has several of the same attributes you find in the Ragdoll breed, such as the soft bunny-like hair, neck ruff, being a large, laid-back, friendly cat that is slow to mature. The tail is much like the Ragdolls being long and fully furred as are the large paws with tufts.

The RagaMuffin's forehead or plane between its ears is more rounded than the flat plane of the Ragdoll.

The RagaMuffin's sweet cherubim face looks rounded or chubby, giving it a broad appearance. The chin should be firmly rounded. The whisker pad and cheeks are full.

Ears are of medium size, and rounded in proportion to the head, set as much on the side of the head as on the top with a slight flare and tipped slightly forward, as if listening.

Instead of the oval or almond shaped eyes found in Ragdolls the RagaMuffin will have large walnut shaped eyes.

In profile, the RagaMuffin will have an obvious nose dip, giving a scoop impression whereas the Ragdolls nose is more of a slope.

The neck is short, heavy and strong, especially in adult males.

RagaMuffin breeders have used Persians, Himalayans, Ragdolls and unregistered domestic longhair (DLH) cats to broaden the gene pool. According to American Cat Fanciers' Association (ACFA) 2008 Registration rules, either the sire or dam must be a RagaMuffin to be registered as such. The Siberian is the only allowable outcross, as the allowable outcross with Ragdolls stopped May 1, 2010.

When the RagaMuffin breed was separated from the Ragdolls, the RagaMuffin Associated Group (RAG) was formed. Some RagaMuffin breeders tout that their breed is less prone to the heart problem hypertrophic cardiomyopathy (HCM) than Ragdolls.

A new litter belonging to breeder
Melissa Firestone of RockstarDolls Ragdolls

The Mysterious Beginning

Ann Baker originated the Ragdoll breed in the early 1960's in Riverside, California. There are several thoughts about her methods, what cats she used, and why the Ragdoll is such a trusting, relaxed and floppy cat. I feel some of her thoughts were pretty far-fetched but she did start the breed, even if she later hindered its advance in the cat fancy world. I am grateful that the breed exists, regardless of its start.

The exact history probably died with Ann Baker in 1997. We will likely never know all the facts of the breed beginnings due to unknown sires, lack of early record keeping, mysterious claims, and her apparent desire to control the development of the breed.

Ann Baker had been breeding mostly solid black Persians and Apple Headed lilac Balinese before she started breeding for Ragdolls. She also bred what she called Honey Bears and Baby Dolls. I have read conflicting information as to how she bred to achieve these two breeds. I believe she stated that the Honey Bear breed came from breeding a female Persians injected with a skunk's genes or some such story, and that Baby Dolls came from breeding a Honey Bear with a Ragdoll. There is also mention of Cherubim and Doll Babies.

Rovena E. Parmley of Tuftytoes took this picture of what she said Ann Baker called Honey Bear kittens. The three Tuftytoes Honey Bear Kittens (two brown, one silver) were sired by Pooky and dam Silver Cloud

I purchased a pre-owned copy of Ann Baker's book, *You've Been Had, Me Too*. I found it odd how so many of the listed breeds had the same characteristics found in the Ragdoll. The previous book owner included several flyers and articles (see photo to right) including:

- *An International Ragdoll Cat Association (IRCA) Characteristics and Requirements Ragdoll Cats Show Standard* by Ann Baker.

- A photocopy of a newspaper article with photos showing Ragdolls IRCA registers and pets with prices of $150 to $300. One list reads "Cherubim Cats," then under it, a list with "Ragdolls, Honey Bears, Baby Dolls, Doll Babies, Symonese, Manxese, Etc."

- A flyer titled *"Cat of the Year,"* stating descriptions of the Honey Bear Persians. "New 1980 Honey Bear Persians They go limp when held...Lay on back... Thrive on love and attention...All love and personality...Longer and not as matty fur and love baths...Profile of a monkey...All colors including Tabby and Tortie... Looks like Persians but not cat skeleton...Must see to believe...New DNA Experimental." This flyer had stapled to it newspaper articles with headlines reading *"Honey Bear cat part skunk?"* Also Attached was a copy of a United States Patent Office Trademark Principle Register to Ann Baker for the Honey Bear

- Lastly an IRCA registrar, including a second list of what Cherubim cats are. It includes the Ragdoll, Honey Bear, Baby Doll, Doll Babies, Angels, and Manxese. It also lists "Wild Cats, Domestic Cats, Cherubim Cats, Outdoor, Indoor-Outdoor, and Indoor" along with "Cherubim cats are cats that did not get their start by breeding two breeds together...one is a phenomena and the others are DNA."

Ann Baker holding Raggedy Ann Kyoto. Photo use and description by RFCI historian Wain Pearce

This may or may not be Josephine. Ann has written on the back of this picture Josephine, most people believe that it is a stand in. Photo use and description by RFCI historian Wain Pearce

The hybrid breed was started with a female cat named Josephine, who belonged to Mr. and Mrs. Pennel, Ann Baker's neighbors. Josephine was a solid white long-haired semi-feral cat, thought to look like a large Angora or Balinese. Some say that Josephine was hit by a car, found on the curb side and taken to a nearby university for care. After her recovery, her litters for some unknown reason were noted for their laid-back disposition, large size, and non-matting hair.

Josephine mated with unknown toms, and had males Daddy Warbucks and Blackie who were half-brothers, as it is believed they were sired from different toms. Blackie from a more Persian looking brown or black tom, and Daddy Warbucks from a more Burmese, or Birman looking tom. I read on pawpeds.com that Daddy Warbucks was sired by Beauty*, but most believe Daddy Warbucks sire is unknown. Ann Baker liked Daddy Warbucks looks and later said he was the "father of the Ragdoll look." Daddy Warbucks was a long-haired, seal mitted colorpoint with a white blaze and white tail tip, that resembled the look of a Birman or Sacred cat of Burma.

Josephine was bred to her son Daddy Warbucks and produced Fugianna. Josephine was bred with her other son, Daddy Warbucks half-brother Blackie, and produced Buckwheat.

*J*osephine's offspring— Daddy Warbucks, Fugianna and Buckwheat are the founding cats that Ragdolls descended from.

Josephine vanishes from this story early. It is believed that Mr. Pennel had Josephine destroyed after Josephine fought with the family dog while protecting her litter.

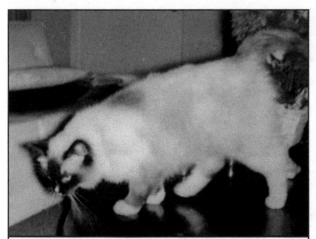

Daddy Warbucks. Photo use and description by RFCI historian Wain Pearce

Ann Baker holding Fugianna a seal bicolor. Photo use and description by RFCI historian Wain Pearce

Buckwheat with her kittens Tiki and Kyoto. Photo use and description by RFCI historian Wain Pearce

Ann Baker acquired both Buckwheat and Fugianna from Mr. and Mrs. Pennel. Ann decided to split the two females and their offspring into two groups that she called the "light side" and the "dark side," making the light side from Fugianna and the dark side from Buckwheat. These two groups had nothing to do with color, but instead with appearance and disposition. Baker thought it best to breed one from each side.

Raggedy Ann Fugianna was the first bicolor. Fugianna had a large amount of white on her long and lanky body like a high white or van pattern. Her inverted "V" that made her a bicolor was high on her face and one of her ears was dark seal while the other ear was white. I was pleased initially that my Ms. Trinity looked so much like Fugianna, until I read that she was poorly marked.

Buckwheat was solid black and resembled more of the Burmese look. Buckwheat was bred to her father, Daddy Warbucks and produced a litter of four kittens. Two kittens in this litter were pointed, a seal mitted male named Raggedy Ann Kyoto and a seal colorpoint female, named Raggedy Ann Tiki. I found Tiki listed as seal in most places and chocolate in others. This litter, born in the summer of 1965 would be the first litter of Ragdolls. Kyoto and Tiki were said to have the coloring Baker wanted to focus her attention on to continue the line. The other two kittens were solid, one solid black male was named Gueber, and the black mitted male was named Mitts. Supposedly Baker originally called Gueber and Mitts along with their offspring "experimental Persians" until later deciding to call them "Ragdolls Tu" but they were never registered as Ragdolls. Some say Baker called solid, self-colored cats or cats with aqua eyes "Miracle Ragdolls."

In 1965 the National Cat Fanciers' Association (NCFA) recognized the Ragdoll. On December 30, 1966 the first four Ragdolls were registered with NCFA. Kyoto and Tiki

B'wana and Woo Wong.
Photo use by RFCI historian Wain Pearce

Ann Bakers Grandson Greg Guess with Kyoto. Photo use and description by RFCI historian Wain Pearce

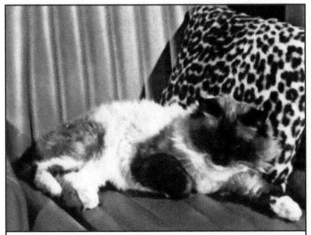

Raggedy Ann Kyoto. Photo use and description by RFCI historian Wain Pearce

were registered with Baker as the owner and breeder. Baker registered Daddy Warbucks, and Fugianna with Mrs. Merle Pennel being the breeder, and herself as the owner. Ann Baker was granted a franchise patent in 1975 that she later dissolved in 1976. Her Ragdolls were sold with strict franchise rules that required registering in Baker's own registry, the IRCA that she founded in 1971. Baker even gave tours of her cattery, *Raggedy Ann*, for a fee.

Baker sold the first breeding pair Raggedy Ann Buddy, a male seal colorpoint, and Raggedy Ann Rosie, a seal point mitted female, to Denny and Laura Dayton in 1969. They called their cattery *Blossom-Time*. From 1971 through 1972 the Daytons acquired several Ragdolls from people that had originally bought from Ann Baker. In the early 1970's the Daytons had eighteen of Ann Baker's *Raggedy Ann* Ragdolls. In 1975 the Daytons founded the Ragdoll club, The Ragdoll Society. In 1978 the Ragdoll Club would become the Ragdoll Fanciers Club (RFC) and then the Ragdoll Fanciers Club International (RFCI). They promoted the breed until they retired in 1982, after thirteen years. The Daytons started a genetic chart that was continued by Charlie Meyers. It is still used today.

In 1973 Blanche Herman bought a breeding pair of Ragdolls from Ann Baker. Bam Bam, was a blue mitted male, and Pebbles, a seal mitted female. Shortly after purchasing those two, she added four more. Her cattery was called *Ragtime*. Blanche Herman was active in promoting the Ragdoll breed.

The Daytons are responsible for introducing the breed to the United Kingdom, when in the early 1980's they sold the majority of their Ragdolls in England to LuLu Rowley and Pat Brownsell. Lulu Rowley's cattery name was *Petil-Lu* and Pat Brownsell's was called *Patriarca*. All Ragdolls and RagaMuffins descend from the original Baker foundation stock, founded in the United States.

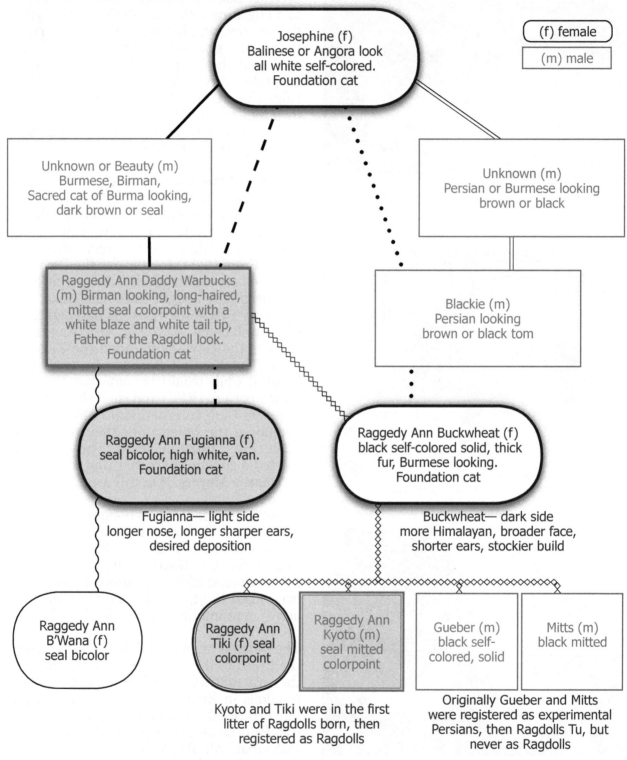

Josephine (f)
Balinese or Angora look
all white self-colored.
Foundation cat

(f) female
(m) male

Unknown or Beauty (m)
Burmese, Birman,
Sacred cat of Burma looking,
dark brown or seal

Unknown (m)
Persian or Burmese looking
brown or black

Raggedy Ann Daddy Warbucks
(m) Birman looking, long-haired,
mitted seal colorpoint with a
white blaze and white tail tip,
Father of the Ragdoll look.
Foundation cat

Blackie (m)
Persian looking
brown or black tom

Raggedy Ann Fugianna (f)
seal bicolor, high white, van.
Foundation cat

Raggedy Ann Buckwheat (f)
black self-colored solid, thick
fur, Burmese looking.
Foundation cat

Fugianna— light side
longer nose, longer sharper ears,
desired deposition

Buckwheat— dark side
more Himalayan, broader face,
shorter ears, stockier build

Raggedy Ann
B'Wana (f)
seal bicolor

Raggedy Ann
Tiki (f) seal
colorpoint

Raggedy Ann
Kyoto (m)
seal mitted
colorpoint

Gueber (m)
black self-
colored, solid

Mitts (m)
black mitted

Kyoto and Tiki were in the first
litter of Ragdolls born, then
registered as Ragdolls

Originally Gueber and Mitts
were registered as experimental
Persians, then Ragdolls Tu, but
never as Ragdolls

Foundation cats: Josephine, Daddy Warbucks, Fugianna and Buckwheat.
First four registered as Ragdolls: Daddy Warbucks, Fugianna, Tiki and Kyoto

Ann holding Kookie, Toy Sue, and Kookie Tu, born in 1966.
Photo use and description by RFCI historian Wain Pearce

Ann with Kyoto and his son Kookie Tu.
Photo use by RFCI historian Wain Pearce

It was a slow, long, struggle for the Ragdoll to be accepted for Championship status. First accepted in 1973 by the National Cat Fanciers' Association (NCFA), then over the years, Cat Fanciers Federation (CFF), CROWN, United Cat Federation (UCF), The International Cat Association TICA, American Cat Council (ACC), American Cat Fanciers Association (ACFA), and finally in 2008, Cat Fanciers' Association (CFA). I am grateful for all the people who kept up the effort to promote this wonderful breed. There are several websites and organizations dedicated to the Ragdoll breed listed in the back of the book.

There are breeders that continue trying to get non-pointed, self-colored solids, minks and sepia cats accepted by the cat fancier's standard as Ragdolls. Some breeders who bred Ragdolls in only pointed colors say non-pointed cats are RagaMuffins. Some of the RagaMuffin breeders say they do not want non-pointed Ragdolls being thrown in to

their RagaMuffin class because the breed standard for a RagaMuffin is different from the breed standard for a Ragdoll. Some say they do not want non-pointed Ragdolls being registered as RagaMuffins unless they are bred from RagaMuffins. The breeders of self-colored Ragdolls say their non-pointed, non-blue-eyed Ragdolls are every bit as much a Ragdoll as the pointed blue-eyed Ragdolls, since Gueber and Mitts were not pointed cats and came from the same litter as Kyoto and Tiki. Solids could be considered "old" or "new." There are breeders of non-pointed cats that can trace the linage back to Bakers original foundation stock. I will say that CFA and TICA only recognize Ragdolls as blue-eyed, pointed cats.

The pointed gene that gives color on the cat's extremities is a recessive gene, whereas the non-pointed or solid gene is a dominant gene. It is possible for a non-pointed parent to produce a pointed cat. However you can not get a non-pointed (dominant gene) cat from pointed (recessive gene) parents. The pointed pattern is recessive and you can not get a dominant gene from two recessive genes. Either the sire or dam would have to be non-pointed (dominant gene) to produce non-pointed offspring.

It wasn't long ago that the Ragdoll was not accepted in lynx, red, torbie or tortie. Only time will tell. Breeders may never agree on coat colors, patterns or accepted breed standards but most will say that the health and personality are the most important characteristics of these large lovable cats. I can say that most breeders I talked with are quite passionate about what they feel to be a true Ragdoll or RagaMuffin and have a definite opinion about what should be registered as which breed, and what should not be. I did wish a few times while doing research for this book that some people's strong opinions were as docile as the Ragdoll cats we cherish.

Karen Wright of Kylador's 37 day old kittens Autumn and Leif (both seal bicolors)

Sandra Baker's Pippin (seal mitted with blaze)

Patricia Besaw's Bellapalazzo Maximillion (BEW, blue-eyed white Ragdoll)

Marsha Harris' Tessie (seal point mitted)

Constance McCarthy's Nicodemus (seal colorpoint)

Debbie Le-Strange's Miwahni Sapphire Rose
of GuysnDolls (blue colorpoint)

Karen Wright's Kylador Samo Sue
(seal point mitted)

PalaceCats Moonlight Dancer (seal mitted) and
PalaceCats Max E. Moo (blue bicolor)

Finding and Choosing Your Ragdoll

Pricing of Ragdolls usually depends on pedigree or lineage, color, pattern, age, gender, and markings (show or pet quality). Sometimes you can find a retired stud or queen that would make a wonderful pet. I personally love the kitten stage but that isn't the best choice for every owner. When I was looking for pet quality Ragdolls in 2007, before I decided to adopt through a rescue, the price ranged from $500. to $850. each. Some breeders did give discounts for buying more than one.

Constance McCarthy's Nicodemus (seal colorpoint) 10 months old and Ezekiel (seal mitted) 14 weeks

Finding a list of breeders is easy with the internet or magazines such as *Cats USA*, but choosing a good breeder from a list is hard work. A good place to start would be asking other Ragdoll owners if they are happy with the breeder they chose.

If you attend cat shows you can often find Ragdoll breeders to talk with and see their cats. You are not guaranteed to find Ragdolls in a show but you are more likely to find them at shows by The International Cat Association (TICA). At shows always ask if it is a good time to chat with people showing their cats, as they may be waiting to hear their call to the show ring. You can find upcoming show calendars in magazines such as *Cat Fancy* or *Cats Magazine* and online by Googling cat fancier shows or at:
cfa.org/exhibitors/show-schedule.html
ticamembers.org/calendar
acfacat.com/show_schedule.htm

Karen Wright of Kylador's kittens

I have had the opportunity to go to a few cat shows. The amount of Ragdolls shown varied from none, to close to a dozen. Before you go to a show, you can call and ask the entry clerk if Ragdolls are being shown. I enjoy seeing so many different breeds in

Ragdolls at a show I went to in Simpsonville, South Carolina in 2009, by *Ocicats International* (CFA)

From the *Foothills Feline Cat Club* show in Shelby North Carolina, in 2011

My Tyler with his beloved catnip banana

Bridlepath Mercedes of Kylador "Sadie" with her kittens Leif and Autumn (all seal bicolors)

person. I was finally able to see a Birman, Snowshoe, and several other breeds I admire like the Maine Coon, Norwegian Forest, Siberian, Bengal, Egyptian Mau, Ocicat, Toyger, Turkish Angora, Somali, long-haired Selkirk Rex and long-haired LaPerm. I would still like to see a purebred RagaMuffin, Savannah, and a Pixiebob.

As a novice, I did read enough to know I was not allowed to touch or ask to pet the cats, even though I would have loved to snuggle all of them. I appreciate the exhibitors that clearly labeled their show cages as to the breed of the cat so you could just read it without bothering them. I didn't understand the show rings at first. I found out later all I had to do was buy a show guide. At some shows you can find an ambassador to answer your questions. Some judges talk about what they are doing when they are judging and I found that more interesting than the ones that just handled a cat, and put it back, and went on to get the next one. Cat shows are often great places to find sturdy cat trees and unique cat toys and gifts. A favorite at our house is a catnip filled banana and a honeysuckle pouch. Both were bought at a show and seem to have a stronger smell or better catnip that my cats love.

It is common for breeders not to let their kittens go to their new home until they are at least twelve to sixteen weeks old. Ragdolls are typically good around responsible children and other pets. Ragdolls are generally gentle cats and lack the fear that would enable them to survive outside. Several breeders state in their contracts that their Ragdolls must be kept indoors-only.

Breeders do vary on what their standard practices are. Always clarify a contract; ask your questions before proceeding, and get a receipt for deposits paid with payment details understood and clearly spelled out.

I know it is hard not to rush and get a Ragdoll from the first place you find one or

Sandy Baker's Holly the Hungarian Vizsla with Rocky

Sandy Baker's Nicky the Dalmatian with Pippin

Kylador's Paige the Golden Retriever with Basil

Kylador's Murphey with a seal mitted kitten

Gloie Wall's Jamie the Sheltie with Katie

Krista Tulle's Chance the chocolate Lab with Zeus

to sign the contract without really reading it, but I truly recommend gathering information and taking your time. You are going to be responsible for the cat's welfare for possibly the next twenty years. The more you look into the breed and breeders you will be able to ask the questions that are most important to you. If you feel like the breeder is holding something back— walk away.

*T*here are plenty of helpful breeders that want you to be as perfect of a fit for their cat, as you want your new Ragdoll to be to your family.

Your Ragdoll breeder should be able to share your cat's pedigree back three to five generations.

You may want to make a list of questions to ask breeders you are considering purchasing from. Here is a list of questions I compiled that were important to me. Some questions are just to fill a curiosity or find out how dedicated or involved a breeder is, and would not necessarily be a deciding factor for choosing a breeder.

- Can I see your cattery?

- Do you allow potential clients to speak with previous clients? Can I get a reference list of past clients to contact?

- How many generations are documented that you can show me?

- If it is not possible to meet the kittens' parents in person, can I see photos?

- How long have you been breeding Ragdolls? What colors? Patterns?

- Why did you choose Ragdolls to breed and do you breed any other breeds?

- Do you breed full time or as a hobby?

- Do you keep some of your Ragdolls for yourself, just as pets?

- At what age do you stop breeding your dams? and sires?

- What age do the cats that you have bred typically live to? What is the oldest you know of?

- Are the studs kept separated from the intact females until a planned mating?

- Are all the studs and dams healthy? Do they have great personalities? Are their offspring's markings often show quality?

- How many males and females do you have in your breeding program?

- Do you allow new litters to intermingle? At what age?

- Do you raise your cats underfoot?

- Where do your cats spend most of their time (whole house, specific room, other)?

- Do you familiarize your kittens with household sounds e.g., vacuums, phones, doorbells, TV, and socialize them with company, strangers, kids, and or dogs?

- Do you show? Why or why not? If you show, what awards have your cats won?

- Do you allow your show cats to be around your kittens?

- What congenital defects are you aware of in Ragdolls?

- How are you breeding to avoid those defects?

- Have you had an ultrasound done on your breeding cats for organ abnormalities?

- Have you tested to be sure both sire and dam breeding Ragdolls have both kidneys?

- Do you DNA test your breeders for hypertrophic cardiomyopathy (HCM) and polycystic kidney disease (PKD)? How often?

- Do you use just one lab or do you cross check with a separate lab?

- Can I have a copy of their last test?

- Do you have a yearly electrocardiogram to check for heart disease in your breeding cats?

- If a cat from the same parents of the cat I adopt is diagnosed with HCM will you let me know?

- Will it be a problem to request DNA testing before accepting a kitten?

- Do you test for viruses? Which ones do you test for?

- Which vaccinations, core and non-core do you give?

- What vaccines were given and at what age?

- What vaccine brand do you use? Is it a killed or modified live vaccine?

- Are there any vaccines that if given would void the health guarantee?

- What sort of health guarantee do you offer (length and coverage)?

- What happens if my new kitten gets sick? What is the procedure I should follow?

- How do you honor your health guarantee?

- If the kitten does die of an illness within the health guarantee time is a necropsy required to get a refund or replacement?

- Do you have any stipulations in your contract e.g., indoors-only, declawing, return to breeder clause or must I take my new Ragdoll to my vet within a certain time frame?

- Where do you register your cats (TICA, CFA etc)?

- Do you send the kitten's pedigree and or registration papers when I adopt a kitten to the registrar or do you give them to me to register?

- What is included in the price? Is there a discount for buying more than one kitten?

- At what age do you allow kittens to go to their new home?

- Are they altered (spayed or neutered) before they are allowed to go to their new homes?

- Am I required to have them altered and provide proof to get their registration papers?

- What if a kitten gets adopted and the customer is unhappy with a kitten, what do you do?

- If buying locally: What local vet do you use? Do you feel that vet is familiar with the Ragdoll breed?

- What are the kittens and adults fed?

- What brand of litter do you use?

- Do you send photos of my kitten, news or updates as I wait for my new kitten?

- Will my kitten come with a care package? What is in the care package?

Most breeders will ask that you only visit one cattery per day and that you remove your shoes and wash your hands when visiting. This is nothing against you personally— it is to keep their cats from contracting other diseases that can be spread by contact.

Some breeders will not let a kitten go to a home with certain other pets (even other breeds of cats), that they feel are aggressive, very young children or a home that does not plan to keep the Ragdoll indoors-only. A breeder who cares about their cat's well being will be interviewing you, as much as you are interviewing or qualifying them.

Nancie East's German Shepherd Shea with O'Malley, who set Shea in her place the first night

Not all breeders DNA check for HCM or PKD, However one of the breeders in the Yahoo! group even goes the extra mile to have an ophthalmologist check her light colored cats such as creams and lilacs, for pupillary light reflexes (PLR) and for stromal iris hypoplasia that is similar to the albino gene.

Many breeders offer a "return to breeder" clause that states if you cannot keep your cat for any reason, that you will return it to the breeder. Unfortunately, with the economy the way it is, more full bred registered cats are finding themselves in shelters. No good breeder wants their cat surrendered to a shelter.

I suggest actually reading the contract. I know, I don't like all that legal stuff either but by signing it, you are agreeing to the terms of it. Some contracts say you have to take the cat to your vet within a certain time frame, some say you must keep the cat indoors (which I feel all cats should be regardless of the breed), others may have a declaw or tendonectomy surgery forbidden clause, and the details of their guarantee of health. Some may require a necropsy (feline version of an autopsy) be performed if your cat dies, for the breeder to stand behind their health guarantee.

Most breeders will not vaccinate until a

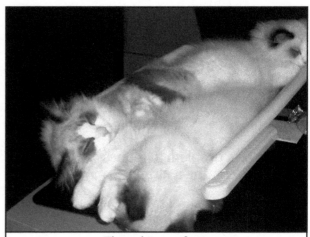

Three kittens from Kylador Canadian Chloe on a scale

kitten is at least eight weeks old or weighs over a certain amount (varies by breeder). Some contracts are made void if you give certain vaccines. Check to see if your cat will be vaccinated before you get it and at what age they give vaccines. You should receive a list of test results, all medical records including vaccines, dewormers or flea products administered with the dates.

A kitten gets antibodies in the pre-milk fluid called colostrum. Colostrum is only present in the mother's milk for the first few days but the antibodies will stay with the kitten for six to eight weeks and will actually make a vaccine inactive if given during those early weeks. More than likely you will not have to worry about the first set of vaccinations because at that age the kitten will still be with the breeder. Several breeders say that the Ragdoll breed is sensitive to certain vaccines and it will be in your contract not to give those vaccines, or if you are allowed to give them, it may specify that they be a killed or modified vaccine only.

Ask if your cat will be altered (spayed or neutered) before you bring it home. Most will agree that your pet should be altered unless you have purchased a Ragdoll for the purpose of breeding. Altered cats seem to have fewer health issues, less spraying

Some breeders will keep you up-to-date with photos and information while you wait for your Ragdoll. Many work on a waiting list. I personally would not buy from a breeder that did not let me visit their cattery to see how the cats were raised and meet the cat's parents. Understand that the nursery may be off limits or that young litters may be kept in cages and separate from other litters for health and safety reasons. Male cats, or studs used for breeding are often caged or housed in a separate area for obvious reasons such as unwanted mating, aggression toward other males and urine spraying. I would want my kittens raised in a home environment

Kylador Canadian Chloe with her litter

Gloie Wall's Katie (seal point) out on the deck

problems, aggression and territory issues. That in itself leads to debate about early spay (ovariohysterectomy) and neuter (castrating), and what age and weight it should be done.

Most pet quality Ragdolls will either be altered before you take them home or come with an agreement that you have it done by a certain age. Some breeders let their cats go before they are altered but withhold the cat's papers until proof is provided they were altered. The amount of vaccines, testing, whether the cat has been altered, show quality, pet quality or a breeder, and the linage— can all affect the price.

as soon as they were old enough to be with the other kittens and cats. My cats are part of the family and I would want them raised that way. I don't believe in caging pets from birth until they go to their forever homes— it seems a little too "puppy mill" for me. I would want my kittens to be familiar with normal household noises and be litter boxed trained when I get them.

I think a lot of Ragdoll owners end up owning more than one, even if that was not the original plan. After owning a single domestic longhair (DLH) for seventeen years, I knew I wanted to go with a male and female sibling pair. I feared that having two could make them not want to cuddle with me if they had each other, but nothing could be further from the truth in our home. Tyler and Trinity both look for lap and cuddle time. In fact, if they were any needier, I wouldn't get anything done. There is plenty of debate whether a male or female is more affectionate and what makes the best living arrangement, two females, two males, one of each or a multi-cat household. The more people you ask the more opinions you will get.

Many people end up purchasing their Ragdoll from a breeder who is not local. Even though the number of Ragdoll breeders is increasing, you may feel more comfortable or prefer a breeder that does not happen to live near you. Even if you need to have your Ragdoll shipped to you, it is still wise to visit the cattery to choose your cat and see the facilities. Ask your breeder if they will ship, use a delivery service, fly or drive your Ragdoll to you themselves. Some require that you pick up your cat in person. Knowing ahead of time when and how you are going to get your new cat home is better discussed ahead of time so both parties avoid a misunderstanding.

Most breeders provide a care package of sorts to make the transition for the cat to its new home easier. It may be a toy or blanket your kitten has used. A breeder on one of the Yahoo! groups even gives a CD with your kitten photos or video. I think that is a marvelous idea— one I would be grateful to receive.

Having a good relationship with your breeder is not just valuable before you purchase your Ragdoll; a continued relationship can be rewarding for both of you. Most breeders say they value the continued contact and hearing about their cats. A good relationship is a source of help and information to each of you, and should a health concern arise, you won't feel as awkward calling them.

You also have the option of forgoing a traditional Ragdoll breeder. A rescue organization or shelter is also an option. You are more likely to find older cats that have been surrendered than you are kittens.

My two kittens came from a shelter, with the agreement that I would have them altered when they were old enough. Part of my shelter fee was refunded after I provided proof that it had been done. Most cats from a shelter are altered and vaccinated before you adopt them. That is part of what your shelter fee goes for and it assures the shelter that they are not contributing to the overpopulation of unwanted pets. It normally costs considerably more for an individual to have a pet altered than it does a breeder or shelter, plus you have the concern of your cat having surgery and the complications it can entail after you are attached to your cat.

We had our first cat, Skeamer, spayed when she was six months old. She was a single indoor-only cat, so I didn't feel the rush to have it done, until I'd lost sleep listening to her in heat, making that terrible mating call during the night. The vet I was using when Tyler and Trinity came into our lives didn't suggest altering until they were five months old. However, Tyler started pinning his sister down and became overly interested in her around four months old, so I talked my vet into altering them a few weeks early.

With most things in life you usually get what you pay for. My bargain, rescue shelter cats, after health issues, vet bills, vaccines, medication, deworming and altering ended up costing more than the going price of a purebred, registered Ragdoll. They are a perfect fit for our family and I would not trade them for the world, but I didn't get off cheap. Not to say that even if I had bought registered Ragdolls I might have had unforeseen vet bills too, but it is more unlikely. I like knowing I provided unplanned, unwanted kittens, a forever home but if the price seems too good to be true— it probably is.

I strongly discourage buying a pet from a backyard breeder (BYB) or pet store. There are enough unwanted cats, Ragdolls included, surrendered to shelters that need a home and plenty of reputable breeders to choose from. A reputable breeder has taken the time and expense to learn about the breed to produce Ragdolls in keeping with the breed standard. When you purchase a Ragdoll you should get a full pedigree Ragdoll that is, or can be registered. If you buy from an indiscriminating person you may not be getting offspring from a planned mating, health testing, the Ragdoll personality, or linage a reputable breeder can provide.

I know there can be exceptions. My best friend Caroline bought a kitten from a local pet store that looks like a seal colorpoint. This pet store was given the kittens, allowing more time to find them homes than they would have had at a shelter. The pet store was not trying to pawn these kittens off as purebreds and had them priced at just twenty five dollars. I once took a litter of kittens there from a young injured stray, which was a kitten herself who had her kittens under a house we were

building. I called all the no-kill shelters to find them all full and not accepting cats. It was spring and with kitten season in full swing, I thought the kittens had a better chance of finding a home at the pet store than the short time they would have been available for adoption in a kill shelter.

When I was looking for my two cats several years ago, I thought our local shelter could have done a better job of finding cats homes by listing them on *Petfinder* individually. Often they listed them as "kittens" with no gender, age, color, or current picture— or they re-used a picture of pets they no longer had available. I am one of those who could not go in a shelter to choose a kitten, because I would want to take every one of them home.

There are Ragdolls without papers where both parents were Ragdoll cats, but if you want to know that you are purchasing a purebred you should get one with registration papers and know its heritage.

A Ragdoll wannabe or possible Ragdoll is just like it sounds. The cat may look like a Ragdoll but the heritage is questionable or unknown. They may be part Ragdoll but with most owners of purebred Ragdolls having their pets altered and kept indoors-only, that is unlikely.

My Ragdoll wannabes Tyler and Trinity from a shelter that I found through a Ragdoll rescue site

My friend Caroline's pet store find, Angel who resembles a seal colorpoint

Watch me grow

Karen Wright of Kylador gives us a rare breeder's perspective of the day to day growth on the next few pages. This page Kylador Canadian Chloe a blue bicolor, with her litter of five. Photos: Top left is the day before her due date, Top right is the day before the five babies were born. Bottom right is birth day.

10/3
10/5
10/7
10/10
10/4
10/6
10/8
10/9
10/13
10/16
10/12
10/14
10/14
10/15
10/17

On this page Bridlepath Mercedes of Kylador "Sadie" gives birth to Leif and Autumn— both seal bicolors like their mom.

10/18
10/20
10/22
10/23
10/25
10/30
11/4
11/12
11/25
11/8
1/1
11/4

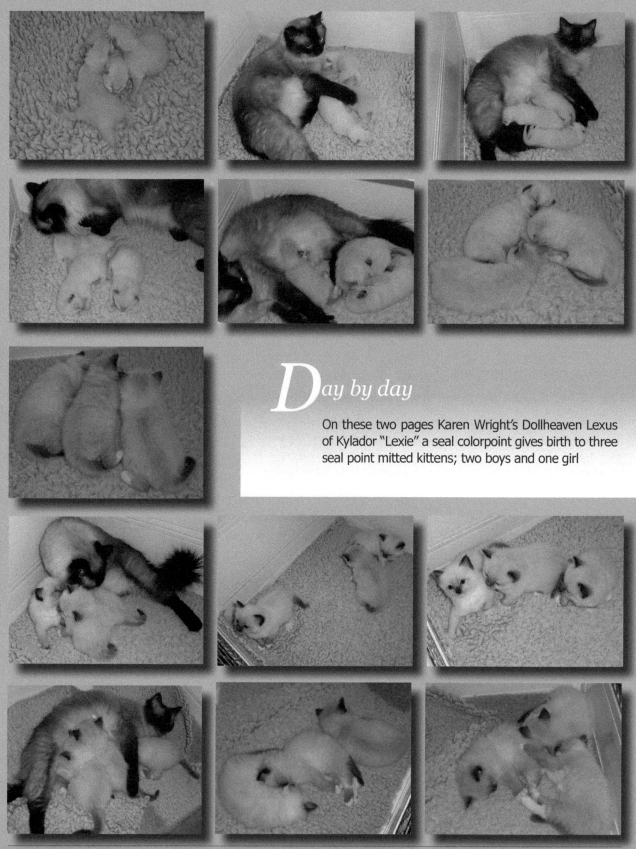

Day by day

On these two pages Karen Wright's Dollheaven Lexus of Kylador "Lexie" a seal colorpoint gives birth to three seal point mitted kittens; two boys and one girl

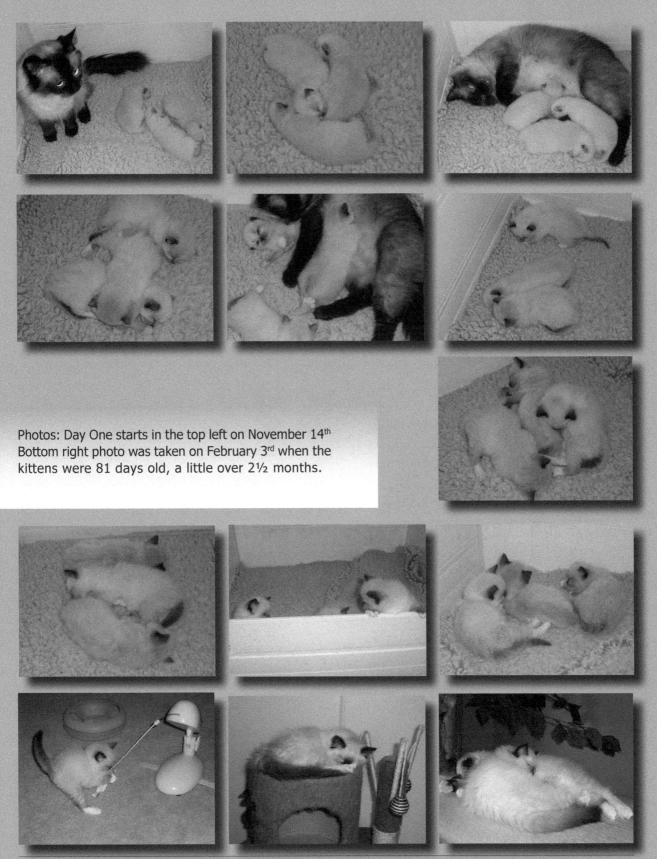

Photos: Day One starts in the top left on November 14th
Bottom right photo was taken on February 3rd when the
kittens were 81 days old, a little over 2½ months.

Gloie Wall's Jamie the Sheltie
with Benji (flame point mitted lynx)

Bringing Your Ragdoll Home

Kylador Samo Sue (seal point mitted)

Sonja Phillip's Brody (seal bicolor)
and Cody Blue (blue colorpoint)

Kylador's kittens (both seal bicolors)

Prepare for the big day by kitten or cat-proofing your home and getting all the necessary items beforehand, so you can spend the time with your new cat instead of shopping. Good items to have are food bowls that are not plastic (see the chapter "Food") food, litter box, litter, litter scoop, carrier, harness or collar, washable pet bed, cat tree, sturdy scratching post, combs, brushes, nail clippers, toys (see the chapter "Toys and Trees"), emergency and first aid kits. See the chapter "Dangers and Emergencies" for more on cat-proofing, and kits.

If you plan on changing the cat's food or litter, do so gradually. Ask the breeder, shelter or previous owner what they used and slowly change over to what you prefer. Your new cat is going through enough changes coming to a new home and will handle it better, the more you keep things the same. Cats can get upset tummies simply from the stress of change.

To ease stress, you may want to purchase a pheromone spray or plug-in like *Comfort Zone* or *Feliway*. These products are made to calm a stressed pet. They are a synthetic version of the same pheromone scents your cat releases when it rubs its face against something, someone or another pet. When your cat smells it, the theory is that it will rub its face over the area, releasing its own scent, which helps it feel calm and familiar with the environment. Herbal flower essences like *Bach's Rescue Remedy for Pets*, olive, quacking grass, impatiens or Star of Bethlehem may help with the transition. Check with your vet before use.

When the big day comes to pick up your cat you should do a visual inspection to make

Bicolor kitten from Kylador Canadian Chloe's litter comfy with the carrier. Linda Dicmanis' Schniffley (seal colorpoint) checking out the flowers and Gloie Wall's Benji (flame point mitted lynx) escaping over the pet gate

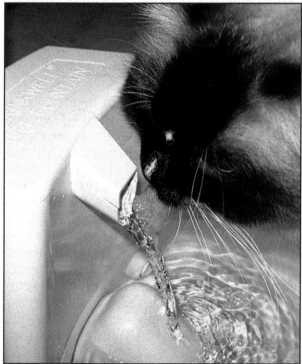

Sandy Baker's Pippin (seal mitted with blaze) drinking water from the *Drinkwell* pet fountain

sure that its eyes, nose and ears are clean with no discharge or smell, no sneezing or coughing, no fleas or pot belly present. It should have a healthy coat with no signs of diarrhea. Look for residue of diarrhea in its britches hair around its backside and legs.

It is a good idea to take your newcomer to your own vet soon, before introducing it to your other pets. I have heard of several cats having upper respiratory problems after you get them home. Many cats have feline herpes. It is not transferable to humans but under stress it can flare-up and cause runny eyes, a runny nose and sneezing. Giving L-lysine to my cats was recommended. L-lysine is used to suppress the herpes virus and boost the immune system.

There are some great books with articles about introducing a cat or kitten to your home. I like Pam Bennett's book, *Think Like A Cat*. The point is to go slow, slowly

Gloie Wall's Katie (seal colorpoint) enjoying the cat tree. RaggleRock Tia Maria (seal lynx bicolor) of RocknRagz playing. Karen Wilkinson's Gizmo and Fred (both cream bicolors) playing ball.

increasing the range your new cat is allowed in your home, contact with other pets and people. Give your new cat places to hide and feel secure and let it come to you and your family on its own time schedule. After your newcomer eats, you should show it again where the litter box is located. Remember it is a big adjustment, especially for a kitten in a big new space.

*I*f *you have other pets,*

make sure you continue to

show them love and attention.

Try feeding your existing pets treats when they are near your new cat, so they associate good things with being around it. You do not want them to be jealous or feel like they are being replaced by a newer,

Jenny Moylan's Shiloh (flame bicolor) with a non-Ragdoll kitten

younger or more wanted pet. How your new cat is introduced to your home is so important.

Children or adults who do not know the proper way to handle a cat should be taught how to pick up a cat correctly. Since Ragdolls are large cats it is even more important to support their weight when you pick it up. An adult cat should never be picked up by the back of the neck or under the arms. Even though Ragdolls often do the "Ragdoll-flop," they may not like to be carried like a baby on their back. You should support your cat when you pick it up with one hand under its chest and one under the hind legs and carry it against your body so it feels secure. My Tyler likes to be cuddled but he really does not like to be carried. The minute he starts squirming or pushing against us, it is best to set him down, before he jumps. Learning your cat's signals, as to when it wants to be put down or does not want to be picked up at all, are important. If you look for the signs your cat gives, with their sounds, body language, ears, and tail— it becomes as clear as if they told you what they were feeling.

Karen Wright of Kylador's two kittens in a cat tree cubby hole

Karen Wright of Kylador's bicolor, Leif

Laurie Nicholson's Rory (flame point mitted) with a RocknRagz bicolor kitten

Karen Wright of Kylador's Ragdolls

Sandy Baker's Rocky (seal lynx mitted)
and Pippin (seal mitted with blaze)

Sandy Baker's Rocky (seal lynx mitted)
playing with an interactive wand toy

Mary Becker's Tedrick "Teddy" (seal lynx mitted)
Toulouse "Touie" (blue point mitted with small blaze)

Kylador's kittens

Karen Wright of Kylador's two kittens

Constance McCarthy's Nicodemus (seal point)
11 months and Ezekiel (seal mitted) 14 weeks

Ms. Trinity Paige and Mr. Tarheel Tyler.
My wannabe Ragdoll, siblings

My Furbabies

Skeamer

Mr. Tarheel Tyler

Ms. Trinity Paige

We had no intention of getting kittens so soon after losing Skeamer, our first cat that we had for seventeen years. We planned a big vacation after years of forgoing one because she needed daily medication the last several years of her life.

It wasn't long before the empty house started to get to me. Friends of ours had a purebred female Ragdoll and we both knew we liked the breed. I made an account on Petfinder.com and joined a Ragdoll rescue list at freewebs.com/ragdollrescue both websites can alert you to Ragdolls and possible Ragdolls available. *PetFinder* even emails you if they find a match with what you said you were looking for.

Since Ragdolls are a relatively new breed, they are harder to find than breeds that have been around longer, plus I was incredibly specific in what I was seeking. I wanted young sibling kittens, one boy and one girl, and one to be a seal bicolor. I needed them to not look like my beloved Skeamer we had recently lost. I did not want a lynx or mitted because I didn't want to feel like I was replacing her. I was not expecting an email anytime soon. Call it destiny if you want to, but my prayers were answered so quickly that I had to find a friend to watch my kittens so we could take the vacation I had planned.

An email came from the Ragdoll rescue site with a link to a picture. Tyler jumped off the page at me. It was as if I had placed a special order, and it had been filled. The five kittens were listed as "possible Ragdoll wannabes." I knew I wanted him and one of his four sisters. When I contacted the foster home for the shelter, she said he was

already spoken for. My heart sank. The *PetFinder* listing said the kitten's mother was a blue-eyed, white calico Turkish Van, with possibly a Siamese sire. Like lots of people, I don't think the shelter had ever heard of a Ragdoll. I will be continually grateful for the Ragdoll rescue website for the listing, and for *PetFinder* allowing people to sign-up to receive emails when they find what you are searching for.

The next day the five kittens were listed in a separate email from *PetFinder*, so I contacted the foster mom again to verify Tyler was taken. The shelter had one application for Tyler, but we were the next applicant. We would be taking two kittens, not just Tyler. The first applicant was turned down. We drove two hours to pick them up. I will say here, not to let your heart get before your head. I took these two kittens and paid the full shelter price for them even though they had no testing, vaccinations and had not been altered. By the time I took them to

the vet the next morning they had already stolen my heart. I needed to know they were not sick or carrying a fatal disease. I didn't think I could bear to return them, but I just could not have another cat die so soon after losing Skeamer. Thankfully the test came back negative, but I was told it was not conclusive at their young age. The vet appointments went on for quite some time with different issues but nothing serious. Four years later, I have two wonderful floppy cats, with only slight health issues that are easily managed.

I feel blessed with my cats' personalities and looks but it is not always a happy story when the background is questionable or unknown. Mine did go through what we lovingly called the "wedge head" stage where their head shape was looking very oriental and triangular – not a characteristic I personally admire. I started thinking about adding a purebred Ragdoll. Thankfully they filled out and I'm happy having just two.

Mr. Tarheel Tyler

Ms. Trinity Paige

Mr. Tarheel Tyler and Ms. Trinity Paige are at least half siblings because we know they had the same mother. Tyler looks to be a seal bicolor and Trinity looks closer to a seal van bicolor pattern, although both are mismarked. Mr. Tyler looks and acts a lot like a Ragdoll with his bunny soft fur. His sister, Ms. Trinity is thinner and has longer, coarser hair.

Compared to a purebred Ragdoll, I can see that Tyler's nose is a little too straight, Trinity is smaller, both have ears that are too pointed, and lack full cheeks and chin. Both have the striking blue eyes and will do the Ragdoll-flop for a belly rub but both of my two Ragdoll wannabes are very skittish and timid around strangers and sounds, which is uncommon in Ragdolls. I mentioned to my husband that none of our family or friends see their true loving, sweet personalities because they act totally different when people visit.

After we lost Skeamer, I pledged to desensitize our next cats by looking often in their ears, nose, and mouth, grooming them all over, trimming hair and nails— all those things Skeamer hated. I even brush Tyler and Trinity's teeth. I am not saying they love it, but I started all this handling early so that they would think it was just part of life. I wish I had rung the doorbell, had company over, and made our cell phones ring more often to desensitize them to those things too. They are even scared of the sound our shoes make on the tile or hardwood, even when they can see it is us.

We are blessed to have these two sweet lap cats as part of our family. I guess I will never know if they have Ragdoll in them, unless I have the Feline Ancestry test done by UC Davis— but it doesn't matter. They are beautiful inside and out and I would not trade them for the world— including purebreds.

I was self-employed when we adopted them, and took them to work with me for a few weeks to watch over them. Many people commented that I had "pretty Siamese kittens" because of the blue eyes and point markings. I think most people think Siamese are the only pointed cats—which of course is not the case.

At first, Trinity was larger, and more coordinated than her brother. We watched them swap dominant and submissive roles several times before Tyler outweighed Trinity and became the dominant cat. Trinity is still more outgoing and will check out company or a new toy first. She is still more coordinated, and she is defiantly smarter than her brother. Tyler is more sensitive, gets his feelings hurt easy and pouts more than his sister.

Trinity wants to play with Tyler but usually only follows through with a mock attack on her brother when she can tell he's not feeling well, but she stalks him just the same. She often antagonizes him and starts what becomes a confrontation. Tyler will get her back but he is never in a hurry. If she bites at his feet or takes a toy, he may let her get by with it, but if we keep watching we will see him slowly following her until he can pin her down, then he simply lays his big ol' self on top of her. Tyler does follow through on an attack which ends in her growling and hissing at him before running away.

Sometimes they will be as sweet as can be to each other, grooming each other and playing nicely and sometimes it looks like sibling rivalry is surely going to leave one wounded. Not only are my two very different from my first cat, they are also quite different from each other too. I had my cats about a year when I was able to sum up their personalities. Tyler acts like a dog, and Trinity acts like a cat.

Both of my cats hate closed doors, regardless of what side they are on. They think I need help on the computer, in the bathroom, filing papers or folding

Ms. Trinity and Mr. Tyler.
Trinity weighs just below 10lbs. and Tyler 15lbs.

Trinity antagonizing her brother

Tyler holding and grooming his little sister

Tyler "helping" on the computer

Ms. Trinity Paige bapping the Olympic swimmers on TV while standing in a play cube

Ms. Trinity and Mr. Tyler sacked out

laundry. Both are definitely jealous of the other, especially of our attention. I told them there are two of us, and we both have two hands to pet with. They often imitate what they have seen the other one doing, which is not only comical, it lets us know how smart they are, how much they observe and retain. Both of them, when they are in my lap, will reach up and gently touch my face with their paw, as if to say, "Hello, I'm here, keep petting me please."

I have heard that cats that watch TV are not as smart as the non-TV watchers, but in our house you'll find Trinity totally engrossed in the movement, watching sports on TV. We think golf is her favorite. I thought about getting them one of those cat entertainment videos, but they have the real thing, watching the birds and squirrels outside our windows. Trinity will be chattering away at the birds when it is just one or two small birds, but if she sees a big crow, or a flock of birds she ducks and peeks at them from below the window sill. Tyler doesn't often chatter like his sister, but the look on his face when he sees Trinity doing it is priceless.

Both of them love to cuddle. Trinity likes to be on our lap facing away from our body but she will quickly leave if she thinks her brother may not approve or want her spot. Trinity is also fond of lying perched on my side, while I am laying on my side. She plays more with toys, typically upside down. We joke that her legs were put on the wrong side. Trinity talks to me after I sneeze. I don't know if it is her way of saying "bless you" or if she's fussing at me for making a funny sound. I will always wonder what happened in the first five weeks of her life because she still ducks when we go to pet her head. I was told by their foster mom, who had them for a week that the place they were rescued from had children that were rough with them and said Trinity was mean. She is not mean at all, but I wonder if the kids were mean to her. Trinity will head-butt us until we pet her, or head-butt furniture and fixtures so hard we can hear it— this coming from the girl who ducks her head. Trinity seems to lack the ability to walk a straight line to us, even if that is where she wants to end up when she's done meandering. She has this uncanny ability to crawl upside down like a centipede. My father-in-law Larry wrote a poem about my cats and mentioned Trinity's "funny ol' backward crawl" in it. She loves napping in any spot of sunshine she finds and is the one I can count on to take a mid-day nap with me. She's a little thief, quick to steal things she deems as hers and run to hide her treasure from her brother. She knows where her stash is, and is happy knowing that her much loved toys are hidden. If I get the toys out from her favorite hiding places, in less than a day she will have them all out of sight again. When I am brushing her, she especially loves to try to grab the hair I've accumulated in a ball. Thankfully I have always caught her before she eats it. I can not imagine the size and mess of that hairball! Trinity often lays belly up or with her legs under her like a camel. Tyler lays with his front legs stuck out in front like chopsticks, or belly up with his legs in what we call his "bunny-boy" pose and he'll kick his hind leg in the air if we don't get on the floor to pet him.

Tyler repetitively jumps at doorknobs, like a Jack Russell dog and he is quick to get addicted to a new toy or game and demand that we play with him often. He has even started running under the ottoman and wanting us to keep rolling a specific red ball up to the skirt edge so he can bap it back. Funny thing is we are the ones running all over the living room to retrieve it and roll it back while he just lays under there waiting. We've discovered he is left pawed and that he would play ball for as long as we will toss it to him. If he comes too far out from under the ottoman skirt and we roll the ball toward him he just doesn't know what to do with it and will get all wobble-headed and scramble back

Ms. Trinity Paige loving a nap in the sunshine

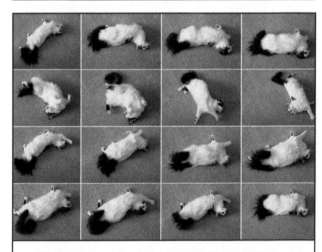

Trinity doing her "funny ol' backward crawl"

Mr. Tarheel Tyler jumping like a
Jack Russell Terrier and playing ball

under and wait for a re-toss. I'd love it if Trinity would learn to hit it back to him so they could play ball together.

Even though Tyler is the dominant cat, he doesn't always have to have the highest perch on the cat tree. Cats are thought to hide their pain very well, but no one told him. If he doesn't feel well or gets hurt, he will let us know. Tyler is a big, sensitive boy that wants lots of love and cuddling. He will try to be as close to us as possible, right on our neck or burrowing half under us. He doesn't seem to understand that we may not want him lying across our face. In fact he gets so caught up in getting

on their laser light toy, the sound will make him gag. He also gags if we stroke a comb with our thumb, if he smells a *Sharpie* marker, or gets near a bug.

They both sleep on the bed— on my side. Most of the time they get in their spots and know momma isn't going to move. I will forgo my comfort to keep from disturbing them. Trinity likes to lie across my legs or ankles. Tyler wants to be between my left arm and body and lies with his head against my chest.

Both of my cats do a few things I had never seen before that I find comical

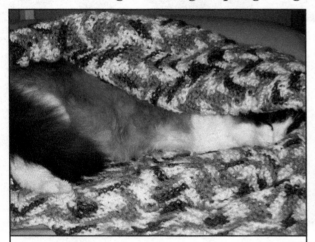

Mr. Tarheel Tyler burrowing in a blanket for a nap

Ms. Trinity and Mr. Tyler both marking the other ones food bowl as their own.

attention that he will drool in happy contentment. Tyler does this head-tilt thing against my body that I absolutely adore. He could do just about anything wrong, and then give me that head-tilt and all would be forgiven. When we make eye contact or call him, he will jump up and go into a happy trot we can hear, that leaves his whole body almost wagging in excitement. He plays Peek-a-boo but does not comprehend that he's not hidden well in the middle of the floor. He gets real low and flat to the floor and then when I say "Peek-a-boo I see you, Tyler" he jumps up and gallops toward me. We discovered by pure accident that if we swing the chain

enough to share. They "kill" their food when I first put it out and they take the first few bites. They will get a piece in their mouth and shake it like they are killing it. My cats also mark "their" food with the scents from their feet by pawing at the ground in front of the bowl. The thing is, when they do this, they usually will go over to their sibling's bowl, and wipe the floor and shelf around the others bowl, marking it as their own.

They know what it means when we say "bedtime" and "breakfast." Although I think bedtime to them must mean time to get water from the sink faucet— instead of time to go to sleep.

Funny characters they are indeed, that enrich our lives and provide unconditional love.

Gloie Wall's Benji
(flame point mitted lynx)

I find that there are more children and dog toys to choose from than cat toys. Check for loose parts or strings on all toys, and check to see what the filling is. Cats should not have toys filled with nutshells or polystyrene beads. Remember to occasionally recheck your cat's toys and replace them when they are old or become unsafe. A good cleaning of plastic toys with simple soap and hot water will help remove bacteria and dirt. You can launder most fabric toys, just check afterward to make sure they made it through the wash and dry cycle without any problems. I used to let Skeamer play with milk jug rings but they are not made like they used to be. Within twenty minutes Tyler and Trinity had it in pieces that could have been swallowed or

choked on. Thankfully all worked out okay, but from now on I will buy the plastic play toys that last longer.

My two, like most cats, find amusement and create toys out of boxes, bags and wadded-up paper. Out of the toys purchased from stores, my cats seem to like the *Cat Dancer* interactive toy the best. With most interactive toys, you need to put them away for safety reasons when you are not playing with them. My two like the catnip mice and lightweight balls, but I usually need to fetch them myself from under the stove, fridge and furniture. They enjoy the ball in a track, pop-up nylon cubes, flat and vertical scratchers, and small soft toys they can carry around, especially their

Karen Wilkinson's Gizmo (cream bicolor) My Tyler, and Alissa Pendorf's Raina (blue lynx bicolor)

Sandy Baker's Pippin (seal mitted with blaze)

My Tyler and Trinity with some of their toys

Mary Becker's Tedrick "Teddy" (seal lynx mitted) and Toulouse "Touie" (blue point mitted)

My Tyler with a catnip bubble

Gloie Wall's Katie (seal colorpoint)

My Tyler and Trinity with the sock toy I made

Mary Becker's Toulouse "Touie" (blue point mitted) and Tedrick "Teddy" (seal lynx mitted)

Constance McCarthy's Nicodemus (seal colorpoint) top shelf, and Ezekiel (seal point mitted)

catnip banana. I have purchased a few toys that did not go over well. One that actually made my cats gag was catnip bubbles. I have also bought some that, for whatever reason, were just ignored. My mom, who doesn't have cats always amazes me with the toys she gets her furry grandchildren, because they are always a hit.

I try to rotate their toys so that they seem new. The ones that are put away I place in a bag with catnip for a little extra zip. They seem to grow bored if they have them all out at once. Sometimes just moving the larger toys from one room to another will peak their interest. As my cats grew out of kittenhood, I added toys with catnip. Kittens act crazy enough without catnip and don't seem to need the herb. Skeamer got quite aggressive with it, but Tyler and Trinity just act silly, so I let them enjoy it as a treat. They also love laser lights, almost too much unless we don't mind playing at all times of the day. If you are using a laser light be sure to avoid letting it

hit your cat's eyes. Tyler has gotten pretty demanding about giving him rug rides on a small rug and both still enjoy a toy I made out of stuffing a large sock with plastic bags and tying the end in a knot (see the bottom right photo, opposite page). They both like to hold this long lightweight crunchy sounding toy with their front feet and bunny-thump it with their back feet.

My Aunt Helen has a wonderful cat toy that is like a kitty treadmill, sort-of like a hamster wheel that her Bengal cats can run on. This would be a great to have especially if you had limited space for your cat to run and exercise.

Your cat should have a scratching surface that allows it to do a full, long tall stretch as it scratches which requires at least three feet of scratching surface. Some cats prefer vertical scratching surfaces, some like horizontal, now there is even a slanted style. My cats like their extra wide horizontal cardboard scratcher too.

Mary Becker's Tedrick "Teddy" (seal lynx mitted) and Toulouse "Touie" (blue point mitted)
from kittens to adults on the same cat tree

My Tyler and Trinity on their first cat tree
as kittens then adults

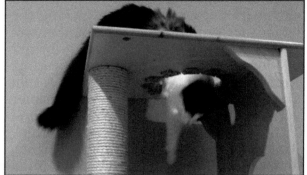

My Tyler on the second cat tree I bought that had
to be returned because it was too small

My Tyler and Trinity on their third cat tree, the *Lotus*

Karen Wright of Kylador's As You Like It "Basil" (blue bicolor) with kittens

I regret not having one or two cat trees around for Skeamer, especially after seeing how much Tyler and Trinity love theirs. Cats by nature like vertical space and want to be up high. Now, I feel cat trees are on the "must have" list.

*W*ith the Ragdoll breed it is especially important that you get a sturdy cat tree with large shelves and openings.

The better cat trees are made of wood, not pressboard or cardboard. They should have a wide base or mount to the wall or ceiling. The tree should be steady enough that your cat feels safe, and have wide enough openings and platforms that they are not likely to be injured jumping up and down.

I added free weights to the bottom of the first cat tree I bought because as my cats grew, they sent it wiggling when they dashed on and off. The weights are not pretty but they serve the purpose. What works for a Ragdoll kitten may be too small for an adult.

I bought my second tree off the internet and it had to go back. The shelves required an almost vertical jump, the platforms and openings were so small, that my big boy could not easily go from one shelf to the other. Some of the shelves for lounging had a post or hole in the center. I only discovered this after taking an entire evening putting it together. In hindsight I just didn't pay close enough attention to the details.

The contemporary and third one I bought seems to jiggle a lot but doesn't look like it could tip. If my cats get any bigger though, the platforms are going to be too small on it also, and I will probably need to attach it to the wall for added stability.

Gloie Wall's Benji (flame point mitted lynx)

If you have the opportunity to check out a cat tree in person, give it the tip test. Tip the tree about three inches off the floor and let go— it should right itself.

The materials used are also important. I have noticed some emitting a strong chemical odor that I would not want to lay my head against and doubt my cats would want to either. You may want to choose a cat tree with more than one kind of surface material to please multiple cats. Scratching posts can be made out of carpet, sisal or wood. I prefer not to use carpet just because I do not want my cats to think it is an acceptable scratching surface.

Karen Wright's Bridlepath Mercedes of Kylador "Sadie" (seal bicolor) with bicolor kitten

Laurie Nicholson of RocknRagz' Rory (flame point mitted)

Mary Becker's Toulouse "Touie" (blue point mitted)

The covering can be attached with glue or staples and can often be ordered in the color of your choice. I think it is easier to rewrap a worn-out post with new sisal than to re-carpet one. I have seen natural tree looking cat trees with post made out of real trees. My cats enjoy the extras like sisal wrapped post and scratchers, along with adequate room to lounge, the top shelf being the most desired of course.

A cat tree with replacement parts, allows you to replace just the worn-out parts, without getting a whole new tree. Most will give acceptable cat weights per shelf. Look at all your options before you decide, and get one you will be okay placing in your home where your cats will actually use it, like near a window, in rooms where they can still be near you and enjoy it. One stuffed into a corner of a room no one goes in is likely to just collect dust. Same thing goes for window perch placement– try to put the perch at a window with something going on outside. It often takes awhile for my cats to accept new furniture, but once they do, they usually do not share well. If they had their way, each room would have two cat trees that reached almost to the ceiling where they could access a cat walk.

Nancy East's O'Malley (chocolate lynx mitted)

Sandy Baker's Rocky (seal lynx mitted)

Karen Wright of Kylador's seal bicolor kitten

Some cats will watch TV especially if you put it on sports or a channel showing animals. Some cats enjoy the movement and sounds. You can also buy videos made especially for cats.

Training your cat can be fun for both you and your cat. In addition to spending time with your pet, the extra activity is good for their mind and body. It is a good idea to teach your cat to come when called for safety reasons and convenience. Many people have been able to teach their Ragdoll to play fetch, sit on command, stay, turn in a circle, give a paw, jump through hoops and even to be toilet and clicker trained.

NenesRags Misbehavn of PalaceCats
(seal tortie point)

Karen Wilkinson's Myst (blue colorpoint)

Cats' tongues are covered with tiny backward pointing papillae, though perfect for grooming, those barbs are the reason that once a cat picks up something with its tongue; it normally gets swallowed. Grooming removes loose or dead hair and mats, which can be painful and invite parasites. It also helps your cat maintain its body temperature. Cats groom up to half of the time they are awake, or when they are nervous or frightened. Some cats can go to the extreme and over-groom themselves to the point of making bald spots. It is thought that this happens out of boredom, stress or a desire for human contact. If this is a problem for your cat you might try crab apple or white chestnut flower essences, after getting the okay from your vet.

Our cats have a grooming routine. If we mess up their grooming order they start all over, and of course, re-clean wherever we touched. I am sure they feel their grooming is sufficient. My two sibling cats still groom each other, but sometimes dual cleaning ends in a catnap and sometimes in a tiff.

With our last cat, Skeamer, any hands-on effort was an ordeal. I vowed when I got my next cats I would start early in their life touching their ears, teeth, feet, grooming, bathing, clipping nails, and looking into their eyes and nose. This just gets them used to being handled in ways they may not feel comfortable with if we waited until late in their life to start. It also gives me bonding time with them and the opportunity to find any lumps or bumps.

As Skeamer became elderly she really needed some additional help grooming her coat, I bought new sets of combs and brushes that she let me use for longer brushing sessions. With Tyler and Trinity, they each prefer different brushes. I have always used a flea comb, and I tried several other grooming tools before coming to the conclusion that not all brushes and combs are created equal. Each cat seems to tolerate the amount of grooming time differently, but I have found that what I use makes a difference too.

Tyler grooming Trinity

Patricia Besaw's (BEW) Ragdolls, Bellapalazzo Sir Bentley and Bellapalazzo Maximillion

I bought a new pin slicker brush to replace my old one that no longer had the plastic balls on the end of every pin. The new brush's pins are so close together, it does not go into the hair very well. Some of the brushes or de-shedders that I use do not grab and hold the hair even if they are great at removing it. My cats are not comfortable outside, but in hindsight, I would consider grooming a cat outside on a leash so the wayward hair could blow away in the breeze.

I use two de-shedding brushes, the *Bamboo,* and *Furminator*. Both remove lots of hair but some people feel that de-shedding combs are too harsh for their Ragdolls. I know that

Assortment of brushes, combs, rollers, hair removers and scissor type nail trimmers

some people who show their cats do not like to use them because the razor blade can cut the hair. Some feel that the cat's coat will become darker, if it is cut or shaved.

I found that my cats tolerate longer grooming sessions, if I do one stroke with the brush or comb, then alternate and pet a stroke with my hand, or give them a natural bristle brush to rub their face on, as a distraction. I try to wait until they are relaxed so they do not see the brushes as a time to play, and I follow a grooming session with a treat. I do not force them to be groomed longer than they are willing, even if it means several short sessions. I

do not want them to dread or fear any part of grooming or care. Cats are often more sensitive on their spine, underbelly and tail. I usually brush my cats once a week just before I vacuum.

Ragdolls typically have more topcoat of longer guard hairs without the thick undercoat and do not mat easily. They require moderate grooming, about once a week. My cat's underarms are the worst area for forming **mats**. If you divide the hair and work with a comb, starting at the ends, and slowly working your way closer to the skin, a mat can usually be combed out. You can try adding a little talc, cat coat conditioner

Karen Wilkinson's Myst (blue colorpoint)
Take a look at that ruff!

or a product recommended in a Yahoo! cat group, *Ice on Ice,* by Chris Christensen. As the hair twists, it will pull the skin up into the mat, which is why if you cut it out, you are likely to cut skin too. If you must resort to cutting it out, find another pair of helping hands. Then take a comb and go under the mat to provide a barrier between the skin and mat with the comb, cut against it, on the side away from the cat's body, using blunt end scissors. There is another product, *Scaredy Cut* Silent Clippers for trimming that I have not tried yet. Some Ragdoll owners have had their cats shaved by professional groomers in a summer cut or lion cut to help remove excess hair.

Cindy Forst's Lili (blue colorpoint) an SPCA rescue sporting a lion cut in a photo composite

Tyler's toenails showing the quick where the color changes from pink to white.

Kevin Wright's Spencer with a lion haircut

Always groom your cat before a bath because any mat not detangled first, will become an impossible mess once it is wet. My cats get a sanitary trim of their long britches hair, with blunt end scissors when needed. With the hair trimmed, there is less to hold litter or remains that should stay in the litter box.

I think the secret to **trimming nails** is starting early in their life, never cutting into the quick and waiting till your cat is sleepy. Thankfully, all the cats' nails I have trimmed have been light colored, so the pink quick was easy to see. There are cats with dark nails, and I can imagine it would be a lot easier to cut too much and cause pain. After I get the tufted hair out of the way and squeeze the paw a little to unsheathe the claw, I can see the color change on the nail from white to pink, so I can clearly see where to trim. You do not want to get in to the pink area where the nerve and blood vessels are. I put my cat in my lap with their back against my front, when they quit looking at what I'm doing and get their head out of the way— I can clearly see. Some people prefer to wait until their cat is napping and then clip the nails without holding their cat.

The sharper the clipper, the better job it does. If you use a dull clipper you may want to file the nail with an emery board afterward. When mine were kittens, I found that regular fingernail clippers worked the best, but as they aged and their nails grew stronger, I changed to nail clippers made for cats. There are guillotine and scissors type clippers. You should keep a styptic stick or powder handy just in case you cut too far and the nail starts bleeding. If you don't have styptic powder, cornstarch or flour can also be used to stop bleeding. I personally would rather cut less, more often than risk causing injury. For your own safety, it is a good idea to trim your cats nails before a bath.

Cats have five nails on their front paws and four on their back paws unless they are polydactyl, meaning they have extra toes. Don't forget to trim the dew claw that is a little higher up on the inside of each front leg. That extra nail does not get worn down when a cat is using a scratching post, and if left untrimmed, it can grow in a circle. If you look closely at the base of a used cat scratcher you can see little nail sheaths that have been removed as your cat uses the scratching post.

I have never tried using **nail caps** to keep a cat from causing scratching damage. The vinyl caps come in clear or in colors. I know some people that have tried them feel confident applying them themselves, and some people prefer to have their vet apply them.

For **bathing**, gather everything you might possibly need before you start. It is recommended to put a towel or rubber mat on the floor of the sink, tub or shower so that your cat's feet are not slipping. One time I moved the mat while we were in the shower and as the water started draining quickly it made a loud sound that scared both my cats, and I had several sets of dig marks on me. Now I let the water drain a little all the time to avoid it making that sound.

I have always given my cats baths in addition to the occasionally needed sanitary wipe, with a perfume-free baby wipe. I am no expert, but I can tell you that with the five cats I have bathed, each acted differently. I find it easiest to just get in the shower with them and use a hand-held sprayer. Some people recommend adding artificial tears or mineral oil to the corner of your cat's eyes to keep out soap. I try not to get water or soap near their eyes or ears while giving them a bath. The most important part is to make sure you rinse well. You do not want any remaining shampoo in their coat.

I buy cat shampoo as well as conditioner, but most of the time my cats are more than ready to be done, and I end up skipping the conditioner. I used to use flea shampoo in

Nail sheathes found at the base of our scratching post

Karen Wright of Kylador's Watson in the tub

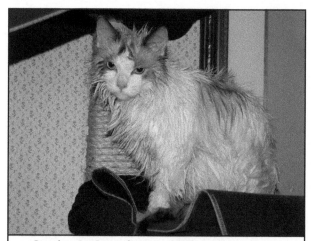
Stephanie Green's Kasseldolls Identity Crisis "Janet" is a blue bicolor, who just had a bath

the summer but have since switched to a topical flea and heartworm preventative. I have heard that a rinse of diluted white distilled vinegar does wonders for the coat, but since I love the clean shampoo smell that only lasts a few days, I have never tried it.

For **drying**, I use super absorbent towels and a hair dryer set on low heat. I also have the house temperature turned up and a space heater in the bathroom. I always give treats after a bath, because even though some of the cats seemed to appreciate the bath once it was over, none of them loved the water or being dried. Skeamer tolerated the bath and the blow dryer the best out of my three cats. Tyler is the only one that was scared of his own wet tail and Trinity becomes virtually helpless.

Some people who show their cats, swear by cornstarch— yep, you put cornstarch on your cat and work it down to the roots, let it sit for a few minutes to absorb oils, then brush it out, leaving the coat fluffy. I tried this once on Trinity. It did make the clumped-together hairs separate and she did look better for a short time. For the feel, smell, powder dust, and short lived benefit of just having her look prettier, it was not worth it in my opinion, unless we were getting ready to do pictures.

I give a **hairball** treat after grooming and baths because of the extra grooming my cats do to themselves after I am done. I have not had a lot of luck with *Cat Lax*, *Laxatone* or *Petromalt* hairball remedies. I will use them but my cats will not just lick it off my finger. I have to put it on their nose or chin to get them to lick it. I have better luck with the hard treats made for hairballs. I also like using flax, or fish oil liquid or capsules containing beneficial omega-3 and 6. I buy the capsules, poke them and squirt the oil on their food. If used too often some hairball remedies with petroleum can deplete the cat of vitamins. I think the omega oils help with hairballs, constipation, as well as dry

skin and coat. In fact I take flax seed omega-3 capsules for my dry skin. It also seems to help with my joints. As much as I believe in asking your vet before trying any feline product, I actually did not ask about it, for hairball use. The omega supplement was recommended by my veterinarian cousin, Dr. Snyder, for Skeamer to help with her renal failure, constipation and overall health.

Ragdoll cats have been reported by some to shed less than other breeds. My cats, especially Trinity, seem to have missed this desirable trait. I have heard from other Ragdoll owners that it is possible for one of their full bred Ragdolls to shed, while

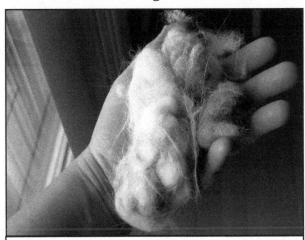

Trinity's hair rolled in to a ball with the *Zoom Groom* after one weekly grooming session

the other does not. Most owners will agree that it is a minor hassle to be able to pet that soft bunny-like fur. Indoor-only cats tend to shed a little year round as opposed to seasonally. Most homes are kept at a constant temperature and have artificial lighting, which only leaves the cat's body to sense the natural daylight hours changing.

Removing hair from clothes, furniture, bedding and carpet is a full-time job at our home. I have several tools for doing this. Most are a rubbery type of comb or brush. Some of the cat brushes, like the *Zoom Groom* are great at getting cat hair off clothes and winding up the loose hair into

Constance McCarthy's Nicodemus (seal colorpoint) and Ezekiel (seal point mitted)

Tyler loves to rub his face on this rubbery brush made for removing hair from clothes or furniture

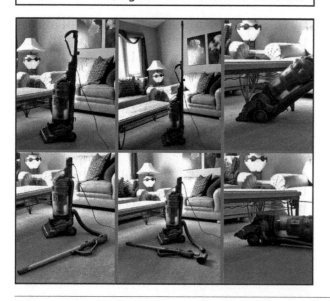

a ball, when I am finished grooming. I try to get most of the hair off fabrics with the rubber brushes or a latex glove first, then wet them a bit, for the second go-round, and follow with a tape roller last. I find leather furniture the easiest to remove cat hair from. Sadly my leather furniture is not free from toenail puncture holes, but it does clean more easily than fabric and holds less cat dander. I have seen several new pet hair remover products, and at some point will probably try them all.

I've learned Tyler likes to use a brush intended for getting hair off objects, to rub his face on; although it removes very little hair. If he hears me using one on my clothes, he is right there to request his turn.

Vacuums... let's just say I have issues with every one I have ever used, and see room for improvement, whether it be a canister, upright, shop vac, pool or yard vacuum.

A vacuum specific for pets or at least one with high-efficiency particulate air (HEPA) filter is a good idea. Vacuuming regularly helps with fleas and allergens, not to mention cat hair. The hair seems to group together in little tumbleweed balls on the tile and hardwood, and is easier to keep fur-free than the carpets. Carpet is probably not the best choice with pets but I do not want to walk on tile or hardwood in every room.

I have a *Dyson Animal* vacuum, one of the earlier models, the DC14. My thoughts and review of it are mixed. I think it does a great job of picking up hair, dirt and dust, but there are some things I wish were different. My biggest complaint is the amount of steps needed to use the suction hose, without the hard wand part attached. I did not realize how often I use the flexible hose until it took so many steps to get to it. The hose is not as long as my *Kenmore* hose and won't reach the top of our stairs. It lacks a light, which for the price, I feel really should have been included. The front is a little too tall and wide to go under the edge of most of our furniture and there is no way to lay the upright part completely flat and still have the vacuum beater bar stay on the carpet, like for going all the way under the coffee table. When the time comes to replace it, I will definitely pick an upright with a canister, but I will consider other brands with a HEPA air filter. There are even vacuums available now with an ultraviolet light that is supposed to deactivate the ability for flea eggs, dust mites, and other bacteria to multiply.

Tyler and Trinity act like little vacuums themselves. If there is something on the floor, including their own hair, they are the first to find it, and eat it. The more we try to run toward them to stop them, the faster they eat it, or run off with the treasure they have found.

I have a small *Bissell* carpet cleaner that I use for cleaning mishaps. My cats come with a built-in trait to run from the tiled or hardwood floors, to carpet, to throw-up a hairball or vomit. Usually there are several attempts, in different locations, before the hairball is deposited on the carpet. I don't know who instilled these rules in my cats' heads. If I hear my cats beginning to vomit, I pick them up and take them to the tiled floor— where they immediately stop throwing up, until I walk away and they start again on the carpet.

You can also try to place a paper towel or newspaper under them before they vomit to help with clean-up but this has never worked for me. We keep carpet cleaner on hand, but the easiest solution is to control the hair before it ends up as a hairball on the carpet. Some people have a hard time telling a hairball from feces but of course there is a difference, even if at first glance that "thing" on the carpet doesn't resemble cat hair. I might add that I've never seen a hairball in the shape of a ball. All I have ever seen have been oblong, or finger shaped.

It is recommended to **brush your cat's teeth** on a regular basis. There are brushes and special feline toothpaste, dental chews, dental wipes, food additives, drops, mouthwash and water additives that are made to help with plaque and tarter. I am not saying it is a well-liked or an easy job to brush most cats' teeth. If your cat is just not going to let you brush its teeth, you can try rubbing a Q-tip dipped in tuna juice along the gum line to help prevent tarter buildup. I have even read that you can give cats the same rawhides that dogs chew on, but I have not found any that say they are specific for cats. I am a little leery of additives that may pose a problem for felines that are not a problem for canines. You can buy dental chew toys, soak them in water, and put them in the fridge for teething. Mine would not play with the cold toys, but they liked them when dry, and that is supposed to help with plaque. As I mentioned earlier, I do brush Tyler and Trinity's teeth; not as much as I should, but I started when they were young just getting them used to having me handle their mouth. My vet did advise me to wait until they were six months old because if they were still teething, brushing could be painful.

Karen Wright of Kylador's bicolor kitten

Alissa Pendorf's Raina (blue lynx bicolor)

As mentioned earlier in the chapter, "Bringing Your Ragdoll Home," you should continue to use the food your cat was fed before you brought it home and then gradually switch if you choose to feed something different.

Plastic is not recommended for food or water bowls because it can hold bacteria and cause feline acne. Bowls should be glass, human grade, lead free ceramic, or stainless steel. Most cats prefer wide shallow bowls so their sensitive whiskers don't touch the sides of the bowl. I use a double set of small *Corelle* bowls for my cat's food and two larger glass bowls for their water. With two sets, I always have a clean set and it gives me extra bowls for special diets or treats. I like that I can put them in the microwave and dishwasher. They do not have the weight or anti-skid rim on the bottom, so I use a rimmed placemat. The rimmed plastic placemat is helpful in keeping spilled water or food contained, and cleans easily. The cleaner it is, the more it seems to keep the bowls from sliding too.

My cats toss the pieces they won't eat from their bowls out several feet into the walkway. The food my cats pick out of their bowl and toss aside could attract ants. If you have an ant problem, and your cats leave their food in their bowls, you may find that a moat type feeder is helpful.

You should give each cat its own bowl and keep them washed and rinsed extremely well, as leftover dish soap can be a problem. I have never had food and water dishes that were attached, but I imagine they would be harder to keep clean. Some think their cats drink more water if the food and water bowls are kept farther apart. I have not done this but it would be simple to try if you felt that your cat was not drinking enough. Water fountains typically encourage water consumption but they do require extra cleaning. I am putting off buying one of those until mine are elderly and I want to entice them with something new to increase their water intake. I think as fascinated as they are with our running

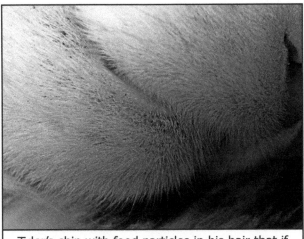

Tyler's chin with food particles in his hair that if not brushed out, could lead to feline acne

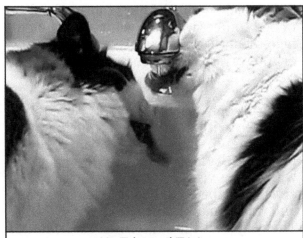

My Tyler and Trinity drinking from the bathroom faucet

faucets that they will drink more water using a fountain.

There seem to be as many opinions about what you feed your cat, as there are choices. Wet, dry, semi-moist or raw; what brand, and with what ingredients can all seem overwhelming. My cats even have a preference on the size of their dry food. If I mixed different kinds of kibble together, like when I was slowly switching brands; my cats would actually pick out and eat all one size or shape, and leave the other. No guessing which one they liked the best! I have found it doesn't matter if I feed them a dry food they love, when it gets down to the small pieces at the bottom of the bag I can forget them eating the crumbs.

In today's market you have labels touting "all natural," "organic," and "human grade." If those words are used in the name of the company, it does not apply to a standard like when the word is used to label the ingredients. "Organic" is legally defined by the United States Department of Agriculture (USDA) to be free of pesticides, herbicides, artificial fertilizer, radiation, preservatives, or chemical additives, but officially, it does not apply to pet food. "Natural" is defined by the Association of American Feed Control Officials, Inc (AAFCO) and the Food and Drug Administration (FDA) to be solely derived from plant, animal or mined sources without chemically synthetic ingredients like artificial flavorings, coloring or preservatives. "Human grade" is not clearly defined legally.

Some people in the Yahoo! cat groups disagree with food a veterinarian may recommend. They say the vet actually promotes dry food diets to pad their pockets with future visits for renal failure, stones, crystals, diabetes, dental problems, cancer, and inflammatory bowel disease (IBD). They say that the nutritional information a vet learns, is funded by commercial food companies, and therefore the information

Karen Wilkinson's Merlin (seal point mitted)

is biased and that your vet will only be recommending or selling food products from companies they make a profit on. This may be true for some vets. With a relative that is a veterinarian, I know she went into this profession because she cares about animals— not making a dollar from a bag of food. She also feeds her cats what she recommends, and I am a firm believer that she would not feed or recommend a product she did not think was good for her own cats. I feel you should know what you are feeding, read and understand the labels yourself.

I know I want to feed the best quality food that I can afford, and that they like. The

Gloie Wall's Katie (seal colorpoint)

Jenny Moylan's Shiloh (flame bicolor) with Indy

best quality does not necessarily mean the most expensive. You have to look at the ingredients. Dog food is nutritionally made for dogs and lacks the proper ingredients for a cat's daily needs.

Skeamer was fed dry *Purina Kitten Chow*, for the first year or so, and then dry *Purina Cat Chow* until around age ten when she was diagnosed with kidney problems, and was prescribed *Hills Prescription Diet Feline KD*. She really could have used the extra moisture from a canned food, but would not consider eating it. We ended up just adding water to her food for the morning feeding, and then putting dry food out, like we always had. Skeamer did

My Tyler and Trinity eating breakfast.
From itty-bitty to adult (note the color darkening)

not see the canned food as something to eat, and that was a big part of the reason I plan to keep Tyler and Trinity, on both wet canned food and dry kibble, so that they will see both kinds of food as edible. It is believed that whatever a kitten is fed and learns at an early age is food, is all it will eat in its later years. I agree firsthand and I have heard from others that making a switch in food for an adult cat is difficult.

I feed wet canned food in the mornings with a little water added, and then free-feed dry food. Everyone has their preferences, but this works for us. When Tyler and Trinity are called for breakfast, I ask "who's hungry" and I swear it used to sound like Tyler said "me me." Of course he quit before I got around to videotaping it. They still get called to breakfast, even though Tyler now expects a personal escort to walk him to his bowl.

Cats are obligate carnivores, this means they need meat. It does not mean their diet is meat only— it just means their bodies require meat and they need fresh water. Cats have a short, acidic digestive tract and an enzyme in their saliva called lysozyme that kills most harmful bacteria in raw food, before the cat passes it as waste in the litter box.

Male cats are more prone to urinary problems that require surgery. What and how often your cat eats affects its urine pH, and that plays a role in urinary health. Pet food manufacturers often add the beneficial amino acid taurine, and keep a neutral pH balance while supplying vitamins and minerals. Pet food manufacturers may also add antioxidants, omega oils, vitamins *B*, *C* and *E*, zinc, beta carotene, lycopene, glucosamine, or chondroitin.

To those who go the route of researching and correctly feeding raw food— kudos to you. I hear rave reviews of healthy teeth, shiny coats, less smelly feces, and

Karen Wright of Kylador Ragdoll

great weight management from feeding raw food. Raw food is closest to prey a cat in the wild would capture, i.e., the whole carcass including meat, bones and organs— uncooked and unprocessed. It seems that people that feed raw food think it is the best thing you can do for your cats. I feel you have to commit to learning what feeding raw food entails to keep the food from containing harmful bacteria, and to provide well rounded nutrients your cat needs. I don't think you should switch sick cats or those with a compromised immune system to raw food because it may be too much for their weakened body to handle the extra bacteria, or parasites that seldom pose a problem for healthy cats.

Feeding raw food requires sanitary pre-cautions while handling the food, and when cleaning the litter box to avoid bacteria found in uncooked meat; which is potentially more harmful to humans, but can also infect your cats if handled carelessly. It is even suggested that if you feed your cat raw food, you should wash your hands after you pet your cat, due to the remaining harmful bacteria in their saliva that has been transferred to their coat when grooming.

After the recent salmonella scare in pet foods, the FDA issued a consumer update that you can read at www.fda. gov/ForConsumers/ConsumerUpdates/ ucm048182.htm. It says that you should wash your hands for twenty seconds in hot water with soap before and after handling pet food or treats. Salmonella is not a problem for most cats, but it takes a lot less to make people sick, especially those with compromised immune systems.

I know that food manufacturers test and research more than I possibly would. Your cat's food should contain certain amounts of protein, vitamins, minerals, carbohydrates and fat. Canned foods are often higher in protein and lower in carbohydrates than dry

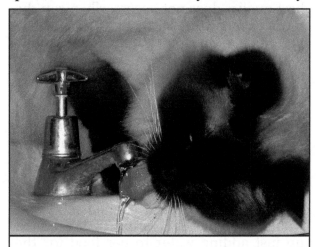

Karen Wilkinson's Merlin (seal point mitted)

food, because starch helps kiblble hold its shape. The higher protein content makes your cat feel full sooner and may help with an overweight cat. Manfactures are only required to list the crude protein or total protein, but that isn't the same as knowing the beneficial digestable protein. Make sure if you are feeding a low calorie diet, that you are not feeding a diet full of fluff, e.g., carbs and fillers. Your cat will likely just eat more trying to feel satisfied.

Look for the AAFCO label. If the food is complete and balanced, it will have a nutritional adequacy statement. A company can make the claim two ways— by chemical analysis or a feeding trial where the food is fed to live animals for six months while their health is monitored. You can read more at aafco.org.

In addition to looking for this seal I would also read the labels. If I were to try feeding raw food, I would use one of the frozen or dehydrated pre-packaged meals that meet the AAFCO standard. I already care more about what my cats eat than how healthy I eat, and our first cat lived a long life eating grocery store brands. Now with what I have learned, I want to make more of an effort to apply that knowledge. All of my choices have to pass the "will they eat it" test. It

Karen Wright of Kylador's kitten

doesn't matter how grand the ingredients are if they will not eat it. I offer a few flavors, by a couple of different companies. I do this just in case the manufacturer quits making one flavor, or there is another recall then I have another to fall back on. I do not want their choices so narrowed that I end up with picky eaters. Choosing this way I feel that I am providing a variety in the type and source of quality ingredients.

Some brands have different food for different life stages. Some manufacturers' list kitten, cat, senior, overweight, hairball, indoor-only and even breed specific foods. Kittens, until they are about a year old need more calories,

higher levels of fat, protein and calcium that you find in most growth formulas.

I finally had to start a chart with the brands and flavors I had tried because I was forgetting if they liked one or not. After I started the list, I realized that it was not just my faulty memory— they changed their minds. I used a range of one to five. One being a hit— they loved it, to five— they walked away and would not even try it. They would love something the first few times then the next time shun the food after just a sniff. My two cats normally agree on flavors and prefer seafood or fish flavors over chicken, turkey or beef. They don't even want cooked chicken, turkey or beef from our people food. I know most vets frown on feeding your cat human food or table scraps. Skeamer ate almost everything we did and lived to be seventeen. Be sure to see the chapter "Dangers and Emergencies" for foods that are toxic, poisonous or can cause harm.

Seafood or fish flavored cat foods typically have other ingredients in it to make it balanced. Look on labels for responsibly sourced fish, or sustainably sourced seafood. Those compainies are helping protect our oceans. Feeding your cat a little human grade tuna is fine on occasion, for a treat, but too much tuna— especially red tuna

Karen Wright of Kylador's kitten

Sandy Baker's Rocky (seal lynx mitted) and Pippin (seal mitted with blaze) helping in the kitchen

can cause steatitis, also called yellow fat disease. Raw fish is lacking vitamin *E*, which acts as an antioxidant. It also contains thiaminase, an enzyme that destroys thiamine or vitamin B1. Cooking the fish destroys thiaminase, protecting thiamine. Feeding high amounts of raw oily fish, high in unsaturated fatty acids, which oxidize and destroy vitamin *E*, causes damage to the cat's body fat, and painful inflammation. A cat with steatitis can become reluctant to move, have a fever or anorexia, and severe pain when touched. Untreated steatitis can even cause death. In cats exclusively fed tuna, vitamin *K*, a nutrient needed for blood clotting does not function correctly. Tuna has a high magnesium content which may increase the risk of stones and crystals forming.

Feeding too much raw liver can cause vitamin *A* toxicity. Raw egg whites contain a protein called avidin, which if overfed, can interfere with biotin absorption. Strictly feeding red and white meat only, your cat may become deficient in vitamin *A*.

Feeding raw food is not a task to be taken lightly. I am not against it by any means; I am just for educating yourself and doing it correctly so you do not cause more harm than good. Remember when feeding raw, canned wet or moist foods not to leave it setting out at room temperature very long.

Recently the amount of bisphenol-A (BPA) leaching into food has come under scrutiny for good reason. It is believed to cause hyperthyroidism, breast cancer, testicular cancer, diabetes, and hyperactivity. BPA and other BP's are used in cans, and plastics, including plastic containers and the liner of some metal cans holding food for human consumption. In my own home I have tried for many years not to cook with, or use items containing aluminum and now we have this concern. I emailed the company I buy my canned cat food from, and they responded that they use it in some of their can sizes, but not all. They say they see no harm in it, but they plan to discontinue its use in all cans. I wish more manufacturers would add "BPA free" to their labels so it would be easy to see at a glance.

When you store dry food or kibble in storage containers, you should use containers large enough to hold the entire bag of food still in the bag, for two reasons: one, unless you buy food-grade plastic storage containers or glass, the container itself can hold bacteria or leach chemicals including BPA in to the food, and two, with the amount of recalls it is handy to be able to read the UPC label on your food should one be recalled.

The Environmental Working Group (EWG) looked at pets' exposure to BPA, heavy metals, and other chemicals. They found the use of non-stick cookware was a hazard, especially to birds, and items such as carpet, fabric and plastics contained carcinogens and neurotoxins toxic to the endocrine and reproductive system. Pets showed higher levels than humans did. This is scary for humans too, but more so for pets as they are smaller, closer to the floor or fabrics, and clean themselves by ingesting what they lick off their coats. You can read more at ewg.org/node/27093.

I recommend joining fda.gov US Food and Drug recall list. You can set it up so they email you or use RSS feeds so you can stay updated of recalls. I joined for pet food recalls but did not see a way to only receive the recalled pet food. I am quite surprised at the amount of items recalled almost daily.

I prefer to feed pet foods that have a high meat content, with no carrageenan, no by-products, gluten or a large amount of grains. By-products can be animal or non-animal by-products. AAFCO's definition of these extras is "secondary product produced in addition to the principal product." The AAFCO excludes hair,

Storing dry kibble in the bag

Karen Wright's Bridlepath Mercedes of Kylador "Sadie" (seal bicolor)

Patricia Besaw's Bellapalazzo Sir Bentley and Bellapalazzo Maximillion (both blue-eyed white)

horns, teeth, hooves, feet, and feathers as by-products. These extras or leftovers can include things a cat would eat in the wild, such as organs, hulls and stems, but can also contain animal waste or diseased animals. I prefer to feed my cats' pet food with primary meat from turkey or chicken as the main ingredient.

The terms "by-product meal," "meat by-products" and "poultry by-products," can all be confusing. The definitions are somewhat disturbing, but what is not said, is just as important as what is. The term "meal," as in "chicken meal," simply means the meat has been cooked or rendered. This processing greatly reduces the water content.

The best idea is to simply read the labels, and continue to re-check them, as manu-facturers do occasionally change what goes into their products. Ingredients are required to be listed in order of predominance by weight. This includes their water content. If it starts with say, "deboned chicken" you are feeding closer to the real thing than if it said, "chicken by-product meal."

Some manufactures have very few ingredients on their labels and they will typically be ingredients that you can recognize and pronounce. Just make sure that it is a complete source of nutrition. The first five to eight ingredients often make up the majority of the product.

The name of the product gives you a clue as to how much of an ingredient it contains. To call a food "Tuna for Cats," for example it must contain 95% tuna. Only 25% of the named ingredient is needed to call an item "Chicken Dinner," "Chicken Platter," "Chicken Entrée," or "Chicken Formula." A shocking 3% is all that is needed of the named ingredient to say, "Cat food with chicken." The word flavor only has to be detectable flavor— a set percentage is not required. "Beef flavor" may be beef by-products or even beef digest that actually contains no beef, just the flavor of beef. You get the idea.

Here is a snippet from www.fda.gov/cvm/petlabel.htm that I feel explains it very well:

> *For example, one pet food may list "meat" as its first ingredient, and "corn" as its second. The manufacturer doesn't hesitate to point out that its competitor lists "corn" first ("meat meal" is second), suggesting the competitor's product has less animal-source protein than its own. However, meat is very high in moisture (approximately 75% water). On the other hand, water and fat are removed from meat meal, so it is only 10% moisture (what's left is mostly protein and minerals). If we could compare both products on a dry matter basis (mathematically "remove" the water from both ingredients), one could see that the second product had more animal-source protein from meat meal than the first product had from meat, even though the ingredient list suggests otherwise. That is not to say that the second product has more "meat" than the first, or in fact, any meat at all.*

Treats often include apparently yummy but undesirable ingredients. Not all treats are equal. There are specific cat treats for hairballs, joints, dental and even freeze dried or recipes for homemade treats. I am not as picky on the treats I give, because they are given much less often and in smaller amounts, but there have been recalls on treats just like pet food.

I have also found that my cats seem to enjoy treats, as much as individually fed pieces of their regular cat food. I do this more for training or reward because they are eating more than I would typically give treats at one time.

Skeamer would take food from our hand. Tyler refuses to take food or treats from our hand no matter how much he would like to have it; he waits for us to set it down. Trinity would prefer we set the food down, but she will lick a piece several times, and then take it from us.

I have attempted to feed Trinity and Tyler their meals in their food bowls only, because we do not want them to beg for food, especially near the table. In the few times I have given food outside of their bowls, it is usually followed by sufficient begging or a cat attempting to stick its head in my glass or bowl.

Tyler is now my faster eater, and before he finishes his bowl, he will start looking to see what is in Trinity's bowl, and will simply push her out of the way and start on her food. I tried feeding her in another room but this seemed to cause stress, as she was always looking over her shoulder for her brother, instead of eating. Now I often just sit on the stairs behind them while they eat, and this is enough to keep Tyler at his own bowl. If I had to feed them different dry food I could see that this would be an issue. Trinity is much thinner and more agile than her brother and I could probably solve this by feeding her somewhere elevated, as Tyler is not a big jumper. This would not keep her from eating his food. For whatever reason, Tyler tends to eat from the side of the bowl closest to him toward the middle, and then starts looking elsewhere. If I see him stop eating, most of the time I can go turn his bowl around and he will finish eating from the side that now has food in it again.

Marsha Harris' Quincy (flame bicolor)

Dangers and Emergencies

If you suspect your cat has consumed a dangerous substance, you need to call the vet immediately or a hotline number for pet poisonings. Most hotlines have a charge that you can place on a credit card.

To reach the ASPCA hotline, call 1-888-426-4435

or visit www.aspca.org/pet-care/poison-control

To reach the Pet Poison helpline call 1-800-213-6680

or visit www.petpoisonhelpline.com

Gloie Wall's Katie (seal colorpoint), Karen Wright of Kylador seal bicolor kitten, then Constance McCarthy's Ezekiel (seal point mitted)

It is a must to cat-proof your home for safety before giving your cat full run of the entire area. My Grandma Erb would have said "an ounce of prevention is worth a pound of cure." Not only does removing dangers before your cat gets hurt avoid costly vet visits, it could keep your cat from experiencing pain, or worse.

Some **toxic items** become dangerous if enough is consumed. Certain foods, or their leaves and stems— are poisonous in any amount.

- alcohol
- avocado
- caffeine
- chewing gum or other things sweetened with *xylitol*
- chocolate— *especially dark chocolate*
- coffee
- garlic
- grapes and raisins
- green tomatoes, tomato leaves and stems
- hops
- macadamia nuts
- onions, chives or leeks
- raw potatoes
- rhubarb leaves
- salt
- some mushrooms

Milk is not good for cats, especially kittens. Even though it is not poisonous, it may cause diarrhea as many cats are lactose intolerant.

Bones found in raw meat are typically okay for your pet to eat, but cooked bones can splinter and cause an obstruction or puncture. I was surprised to find bones in several cans of wet cat food. I didn't know if it was raw or cooked so I stopped buying those brands.

Eve Kurpiers Snuggler (chocolate torbie bicolor)

Shalane Doucette of PalaceCats
flame point male kitten, nine weeks old

Watch how your cat eats *Greenies* dental treats, as they are designed to be chewed and not swallowed in large chunks.

Some cats seem prone to eat certain items not usually consumed or considered edible— this is called **PICA syndrome**. It can be a medical condition where a cat is lacking a mineral, or has an underlying health issue. It can also be behavioral. Some cats suckle wool, but that is usually attributed to early weaning. The intense desire to continue to nurse usually goes away with time.

Skeamer had a thing for any kind of plastic. We could not leave it out, even for a second. I once had to take her to the vet when she unknown to me ingested and was passing the plastic that covers dry cleaning. I didn't want to pull it and cause any damage so I took her to the vet who pulled it without problem.

Shalane Doucette PalaceCats NicNack
(seal lynx male) helping with a scrapbook

Karen Wright of Kylador's Watson

Patricia Besaw's Bellapalazzo Sir Bentley
(BEW, blue-eyed white)

Mr. Tyler and Ms. Trinity

Christmas at our house

Tyler and Trinity bite paper, cardboard, books, magazines, buttons, zippers, tape, stamps, envelopes, and photos. As kittens, they were more interested in items that could pose serious dangers. I have a large carousel with a real horse hair tail. I had to tie the tail up in a pillowcase to keep them from eating it. My camera strap looks like it will always be a source of amusement, but thankfully electrical cords don't seem to interest them any longer. I bought bitter apple spray and sprayed our cords and plants with it. I also tried hot pepper spray, and vinegar water spray as deterrents, but time and age, seemed to work the best. Cord and wire covers are now available like Flexible Nylon Convolute Wire Loom, *Chewsafe,* and *CritterCord*. My two were past kitten stage when I first heard of those ingenious products.

My cats are scared of sounds, and humming is one of the really "scary" sounds. I used that to my advantage the day I accidentally dropped a plate in the kitchen. It hit the tile and broke in to pieces that scattered up to eight feet on impact. There is no way to shut our kitchen off from the rest of the house. I was cleaning up the mess when Tyler came to inspect the situation. I tried telling him "no" and shooing him away. My husband tried calling him but Tyler kept coming toward me. Running out of options to make him stay clear– I started humming to make him retreat. Once the vacuum came out I had plenty of time to find all of the broken pieces. Now don't you know I felt like a fool on all fours, humming to keep Tyler from getting ceramic glass pieces in his feet!

There is the potential to step on, or injure your cat with a scooter or wheelchair. This seems especially true at night and with kittens. I don't know if cats think we can see as well as they do at night and therefore do not see the problem in lying in the walkway, but it makes me do the shuffle-step when I don't turn a light on. We must not be the only people with this problem, as I have seen slippers that light your path as you walk.

Kittens can seem to appear out of nowhere when you least expect them. It is amazing how fast they can move from one spot to another, before you realize they are underfoot.

We had a potential hazard that I had not considered with our slatted back dining chairs. Tyler hung himself by jumping up from the seat and getting his upper body

through the slats in our chairs then as he came down he hung himself in the narrowing opening. Thankfully his back feet touched the seat but if I had not been home, or his back feet had not kept his weight off his neck, he could have strangled to death. I put pillowcase covers over the back of all our slat chairs for months until my cats were larger.

The bedroom furniture was another source of potential harm when our kittens were small. The furniture lacked a covered bottom or dust cover. Our kittens could get under the furniture and climb up in and between the drawers. Instead of adding bottoms to close the access we stuffed big beach towels under the bottom edges to make it unreachable until they were big enough that they couldn't fit. Sofas, loveseats or box springs without cambric or fabric covering to keep cats from getting into the springs is also dangerous.

Our cats could fit through the rungs of our stair handrail, and they liked to go through the balusters and look at themselves in a mirror. Tyler, not being as balanced as his sister, actually fell to the tile. Thankfully he was not injured, but I added a lounge cushion over the tile, and we blocked off the railing on the second floor so they could not

Marsha Harris' Tessie (seal point mitted)

Karen Wright of Kylador's bicolor kitten

PalaceDolls AbbyRose of RocknRagz (blue bicolor)

Dollheaven Lexus of Kylador "Lexie" with kitten

Karen Wright of Kylador's Ragdolls

Karen Wright of Kylador's bicolor kitten

My Tyler

Susan Thompson Dollheaven Tinkerbell and Dollheaven Tallulah

fall through into the stairwell. It stayed this way until Tyler became too big to fit. Trinity can still fit through but we believe she is coordinated enough not to cause injury to herself. We couldn't leave vinyl siding tied to our iron handrail forever.

Common dangers found inside homes:

- breakable items that could be knocked off a shelf and broken. I have heard of people using museum glue to secure their breakables
- cords that may pull the attached item off a counter onto your cat like an iron or hair dryer
- doors that could close on a cat, or pinch its paws in the hinges
- holiday decorations including Christmas ornament hooks and tinsel
- over the counter (OTC) medication, prescription medication including pills, creams and patches, especially those containing aspirin and acetaminophen
- pet medication incorrectly given and some vitamins
- small objects that could be swallowed, including children's toys or parts that could come off pet toys

Other household dangers include:

- aquariums
- bag handles
- blind or drapery cords
- chipping or peeling paint
- cigarettes, cigarettes butts, nicotine and secondhand smoke
- electrical cords and outlets
- essential oils
- fireplaces, wood stoves, and heaters
- hand sanitizer
- match tips
- mold and mildew
- plastic bags

- recliner mechanisms
- rocking chairs
- sleeper sofa mechanisms
- snow globe contents *if broken*
- unattended candles, hot wax, potpourri *especially liquid*
- unsecured window screens

Office equipment and supplies:

- glue
- paperclips
- pencil lead
- printers
- rolling desk chair
- rubber bands
- shredders
- staples

Bathroom, kitchen, laundry and cleaning supplies:

- aluminum foil
- bread ties
- cellophane plastic wrap
- cleaners
- detergent
- dish washing gloves
- drain cleaner
- fumes from oven cleaner
- hot stove tops
- knives
- fabric softeners
- pins
- some odor eliminator sprays
- yarn, thread and strings
- bath oils
- cosmetics
- dental floss
- hair dye
- hair regrowth cream

- hairspray
- lotions *including suntan lotion*
- mouthwash
- nail polish
- nail polish remover
- open toilet lids *danger of drowning or ingesting chemicals*
- perfume
- razors
- rubbing alcohol
- shampoo
- soaps

If a product has any kind of warning to "call poison control" if ingested, says "danger" or "corrosive" on the label, you can be sure it will also be harmful to your pet. The harmful substance does not have to be ingested, remember that cats can absorb dangerous chemicals through their paw pads or transfer from their coat when they are cleaning themselves.

Bleach is a good sanitizer but should be used in a low 1% bleach to water ratio, and it should be completely rinsed and dried before your pet can come in contact with it. *Lysol*, too, should be rinsed and completely dry. Lots of hand sanitizer contains alcohol. In most instances washing your hands with soap and warm water for several minutes is easier on your hands and just as effective. My Tyler loves the smell of bleach. He acts like he has smelled some form of catnip. I do not know what his obsession is, but if I use bleach, he starts rolling everywhere and trying to smell it. I have to be extra careful with him.

If a cleaner has a strong smell, look on the label to make sure it does not contain chemicals that are toxic, like phenols or benzyl alcohol. Homemade or cleaning products containing natural substances like white vinegar or baking soda are safer alternatives. I have read that you can use

Sandy Baker's Pippin (seal mitted with blaze)

Sandy Baker's Rocky (seal lynx mitted)

Constance McCarthy's Ezekiel (seal point mitted) and Nicodemus (seal colorpoint)

baking soda, *Borax*, or *Tang* to clean toilets, but some citrus products can be harmful and contain essential oils. Just because a product says it is green, organic, or safe for the environment, does not mean it could not be harmful to your cat.

The American Society for the Prevention of Cruelty to Animals (ASPCA) website has pictures of poisonous plants. They also have a section of nontoxic plants which is helpful if you would like to add safe plants to your home. If you are like me, and you don't know what plants you own, it is a very useful site. There were over 390 poisonous plants when I last looked.

Partial list of poisonous plants:
- aloe vera plant *not the gel inside*
- amaryllis
- autumn crocus
- azalea
- castor bean (mole bean, African wonder tree)
- chrysanthemum (daisy, mum, etc.)
- cyclamen (sowbread)
- dumb cane
- English Ivy
- kalanchoe (Mother-In-Law-Plant, devils back-bone, chandelier plant, Mother of millions)
- lilies *including Peace lily*
- mistletoe
- narcissus (jonquil, daffodils)
- oleander (rose-bay)
- Pothos (devil's ivy, taro vine, ivy arum)
- rhododendron
- sago palm
- schefflera (octopus or umbrella tree, starleaf)
- tulip
- yew

Remember that closed doors are not always enough to keep a cat out of the cabinet. You

Sandy Baker's Rocky (seal lynx mitted)

may have to purchase child safety locks for cabinets that store potential hazards. Don't forget about what you put in the trash can either, as they are often accessible.

When Tyler and Trinity first came to live with us we really had to be careful when we were going though the door, especially with Tyler. He would try to run past us to get outside or into the garage. I ended up picking up a cat toy to toss away from the door when I was ready to leave. He would run after the toy, letting me out the door. It took a while for the escape attempts to stop but now they would rather be indoors. Filling a can with pennies to shake was also suggested but since my cats are so scared of sounds I opted for tossing the toy. We only allow our cats outside if we hold them on our laps. It seems that once you start letting a cat outside, even supervised, sometimes the cries and pleas to go out become frequent and bothersome.

Leaving doors open to washers, dryers

Kylador As You Like It
"Basil" (blue bicolor)

Marsha Harris' Tessie
(seal point mitted)

BoysnRags Maximus of
PalaceCats (blue bicolor)

Linda Dicmanis'
Schniffley and Bingo

Sandy Baker's Pippin
(seal mitted with blaze)

Mrs. Mary Ewen of
Drouindolls' Song (choc. bi)

Linda Dicmanis Bingo
(blue colorpoint)

Linda Dicmanis Schniffley
(seal colorpoint)

refrigerators, dishwashers, the outside or the garage can all pose dangers.

Harmful garage items:

- antifreeze
- fertilizer
- gasoline
- insecticides
- paint thinner
- pest rid supplies *including sticky traps and mothballs*
- pool or spa products
- rodenticide

A product gaining popularity for cats are **outdoor enclosures**. These can range from elaborate fences with a specially designed angled top for your entire yard, to smaller pop-up tents or window perches that extend outside the windows. The idea behind them is to keep your cats in, and other animals out.

If your cat can come in contact with the **outside**, you need to apply the same precautions you would if allowing your cat outside without an enclosure. Be aware that certain toads, frogs, animals or insects are poisonous, toxic, bite, or sting. An animal that ingested a harmful product, like a mouse that ate bait can be dangerous if your cat ingests the poisoned mouse. The risk of parasites also increases if any of your pets are allowed outside.

You should be mindful of the kinds of mulch, pesticides, plants, fertilizer, lawn care products, and chemicals that may be in your yard or driveway. Your cat could also come in contact with various diseases if there had been a diseased animal in your yard where your cat has access.

There are **pet strollers** made like baby strollers, with the top enclosed in netting or clear plastic that allows you to take your cat on a walk. This gives your cat a view

Nancy East's Murphey (flame colorpoint)

Mary Becker's Tedrick "Teddy" (seal lynx mitted) and
Toulouse "Touie" (blue point mitted with small blaze)

Kylador Canadian Chloe (blue bicolor)

Gloie Wall's Katie (seal colorpoint)

Sandy Baker's Pippin (seal mitted with blaze)
and Rocky (seal lynx mitted)

Mrs. Mary Ewen of Drouindolls'
chocolate colorpoint female kitten

of the outside, without ever touching the ground. It is possible to leash or harness train your cat so they can enjoy walking with you. As mentioned before, Ragdolls should never be outside on their own.

It is a good idea to **locate your cats** before leaving home, know that they are safe and can still get to their food, water, and litter box. I have accidentally shut mine in our closet. I was unaware that they ran into a room while the door was open and closed them inside. Trinity is able to let herself out of a room with a bifold door, but her brother will just stay in there till the door is opened. Trinity has even let us know when her brother was shut in the closet. One time Trinity spent the entire night accidentally shut inside our office. She was so good, but she was ready to be let out in the morning. I bet she wondered why her brother didn't return the favor and let us know when she was the one shut in.

No matter how careful you are about keeping your cat inside, you should use a safety breakaway collar with your identity and phone number on it. You also have the option of having a **microchip** the size of a grain of rice implanted in your cat. There is debate about site reactions, possible increase in cancer and chip readability.

The different kind of chips can only be read by certain scanners. If the local shelter scans your cat with one kind of scanner, it may not pick up the microchip your vet implanted, especially if you have relocated. There is not a truly universal scanner available yet, but most scanners can read the 125 kHz chip and more recently the 134.2 kHz chip. It is a good idea to ask your vet which scanners the local shelters use, and use a chip they can read. All chips are useless if you do not register your information into the database. Some vets do this initially for you but it is up to you to keep the information updated. Microchipping greatly increases the chance

of having your pet returned to you, if it shows up at a shelter.

Even if you choose not to microchip your cat, at least have a **collar with a tag** and bell on it. The collar could be something like a tag from togethertag.com complete with your information. You can buy a special tag and locators like the one by *SpotLight GPS* or *Loc8tor*. The two part device sends a signal from the tag you placed on your cat's collar to the hand-held honing device. This would be handy when you are trying to find your cat, to locate it before leaving your home, or to get to a vet appointment on time. With the recent loss of the cat that got loose from its carrier at the airport after flying in airplane cargo, I would think that a GPS collar would be a good idea for traveling also.

If your pet is **lost**, the faster you jump into action the better. Look around your home, contact neighbors, shelters, animal control, and the Humane Society. For whatever reason, pets tend to go to the right of where they escaped— hide and not make a sound. If you put out "lost cat" signs, remember to leave off some of the details, so that if someone calls, you can ask them about a particular mark your cat has. It's not a good idea to give out money before you get your pet back, even if you are offering a reward.

Pets911.com offers a search box that you put your zip code in to find local shelters. There are several apps available for smartphones and these sites may be helpful in your search, adoptapet.com, petfinder.com, and worldanimal.net.

It is a good idea to have recent pictures of your cat in case of an emergency where you could become separated. My family will tell you that I have this area covered. You should also have some photos online in case your home and photos are destroyed, you can print photos from an online account.

Gloie Wall's Benji (flame point mitted lynx)

Planning for an emergency or the unexpected is important, including having an emergency kit, knowing beforehand which hotels allow pets, and an evacuation plan. There are pet alert rescue decal stickers, like you may have seen for children, available to place on your home that list the number of pets inside, with pet type, and name.

Having paper records scanned and accessible online, with your pets photos, will allow access to them if your original copies are destroyed. In some areas you may need your cat's health certificate or a pet passport.

It is important during times that may be stressful to your cat, to remain as calm as possible. Cats pick up on your emotions. If you are home when a warning or watch is sounded, but it is not yet time to evacuate, it is a good idea to gather your supplies and pets into one room. That way if you do need to evacuate, you can quickly find your pets and get them in their carriers. I find it hard not to take it as a snub when mine are so scared that they prefer being under the bed, as opposed to my comforting arms, but this is usually the case. It would be much harder and take more time to gather them from a hiding spot. In case a disaster should arise when you are not able to get home, it is important to have a trusted neighbor capable of getting into your home, know your pets, their names and where your carriers and emergency kit are kept.

*R*emember that an injured or scared cat can attack even its owner.

You should not try to treat an injured pet yourself— stabilize it, call your vet or emergency clinic, and follow their instructions.

Mary Becker's Toulouse "Touie" (blue point mitted with small blaze) and Tedrick "Teddy" (seal lynx mitted)

Your **emergency kit** should have:

- medical and vaccination records, your contact information and your vets, a photo of your pets, *all in something waterproof*
- a first aid kit
- large carriers or crate labeled with your contact information and your vets
- several days of food, water and medications
- feeding bowls
- leash, harness or collar
- litter box
- litter
- trash size disposable bags
- disposable wipes
- bedding
- familiar toys
- pheromone spray like *Bach's Rescue Remedy*

Be careful using some flower essences and essential oils because they may contain alcohol.

Your **first aid kit** should contain:

- your vets contact information
- poison control and emergency clinic contact information
- list of your pets medications
- vaccination records *especially rabies*
- a list of any major medical issues surgeries, allergies, reactions to medication or vaccinations
- a towel *to wrap and contain your cat in*
- milk of magnesia
- activated charcoal
- clean cloths
- cotton balls
- gauze pads and rolls
- bandage tape
- an elastic bandage
- hydrogen peroxide

- antibiotic ointment *without pain reliever*
- scissors
- eyewash
- tweezers
- oral syringe
- electrolyte fluid *such as unflavored Pedialyte*
- latex or rubber gloves
- ice and heat packs
- digital rectal thermometer
- *K-Y* lubricant or petroleum jelly
- antiseptic wipes
- styptic stick
- flashlight
- magnifying glass
- cat muzzle *for use only if your cat is NOT vomiting*
- simple emergency instructions for performing the Heimlich maneuver, and instructions to stop bleeding

Kylador As You Like It "Basil" (blue bicolor)

Mary Becker's Tedrick "Teddy"
(seal lynx mitted) and Toulouse "Touie"
(blue point mitted with small blaze)

Litter and Litter Boxes

It seems the choices in litter are far greater than our choices of toilet paper. Thankfully, kittens come with the innate knowledge of how to use the litter box. It is partly taught from their mother and part an instinctive need to eliminate in a substance that will quickly remove the liquid, with the ability to cover waste.

With Skeamer we used one brand of clay litter her entire life. She was happy with it, and never, not one time, went outside the box, so I was not about to experiment with other types or brands.

When we got Tyler and Trinity I tried natural scoopable litters made of corn or wheat that were labeled as flushable. This was great when the kittens had diarrhea because we wanted that stinky clump gone quickly. Tyler thought his litter box full of corn or wheat was a big bowl of food, so I went back to using the regular litter until he was older and stopped eating it. It is also suggested to use caution with small kittens around self-cleaning litter boxes to avoid injury.

Litter choices include scoopable, clumping, flushable, clay, sand, corn, pine, cedar, wood based green tea, zeolite, crystals, dried pea pods, wheat, alfalfa pellets, soy, paper, walnut shells, coconut husks, with odor eliminators, scented and unscented, with or without baking powder, some that changes color when soiled and litter

Mrs. Mary Ewen of Drouindolls' Ragdoll kittens: two chocolate points, three lilac points, one chocolate point with one lilac bicolor, three lilac points and two cream points

PalaceCats Isabella
blue colorpoint female

PalaceCats CocoChanel
seal point female

PalaceCats cream
point male

PalaceCats pet quality
mismark seal bicolor

PalaceCats blue
bicolor female

PalaceCats blue point
mitted male

PalaceCats Moonlight
Dancer seal mitted

PalaceCats Max E Moo
blue bicolor male

that can detect a urine pH change or blood, so you know when to see a vet. Some people even use inexpensive chicken feed crumbles for litter.

I found that the corn and wheat litter I tried can attract small moths. I simply put a moth trap near the litter, out of reach of my cats. I like the light weight of the corn, wheat and pine when I carry the bags home and when I clean the boxes. Some of the pine litters I tried were light enough to cling to my cat's long hair on their britches and feet tufts. You should be careful with pine litter if you or your cat have breathing problems or some allergies. I found if I mixed the pine litter with either the corn or wheat it had more odor fighting control and kept it from being as fluffy as it was on its own.

I really like the consistency and weight of *Fresh Results 8 in 1*. It has a slightly funny odor but my main complaint is they do not list the exact contents— other than "all natural materials." I cannot find what is

Lynn Freeman's Dinky (seal bicolor)

actually in it or in addition to the natural materials, so I hesitate to continue using it. One natural scoopable litter I tried, *Arm & Hammer Essentials*, smelled so bad when I opened the bag that I just could not use it. I do like and continue to use their scoopable litter. I emailed both companies but did not receive a response from them.

You can forgo all litter, scooping and cleaning, by teaching your cat to use the toilet. There are **toilet training** kits available. Note that with this method you are at a disadvantage of noticing changes in output and it may be harder for young and elderly cats to straddle the seat.

We should all be more conscious about the environmental impact of our litter choices and disposal methods. The amounts of non-biodegradable and biodegradable litter, which has been tied up in plastic bags that do not decompose, are filling landfills at a staggering rate.

Lynn Jasper's SupurRags Princess Isabella "Bella"

PalaceDolls AbbyRose of RocknRagz
(blue bicolor)

Sandy Baker's Rocky (seal lynx mitted)

Bridlepath Mercedes of Kylador "Sadie"
(seal bicolor) with babies

Karen Wright of Kylador four Ragdolls

Karen Wright of Kylador bicolor Ragdolls

Trexdolls Phoebe of RockstarDolls
(blue tortie point bicolor)

Bridlepath Mercedes of Kylador "Sadie"
(seal bicolor) with two bicolor kittens

Melissa Firestone of RockstarDolls'
seal mitted show quality female kitten

Several brands use silica gel in their product to help its clumping ability. My biggest issue with the sand and clay type scoopable litters is the weight and dust. I don't like breathing the dust when I add litter to the box or when scooping or sifting. I tried several different brands, again gradually switching until I found an unscented multi-cat scoopable litter that I personally like and my cats will use.

Pregnant women should not have litter box duty and should avoid petting stray cats while pregnant. Cat feces can contain the infectious parasite, toxoplasma gondi, usually found in the oocyst or egg stage. If you are pregnant and have never been exposed to the parasite, you can get toxoplasmosis which can be harmful to a fetus and cause birth defects. Infection occurs when infected oocysts are ingested. Costal areas with high volumes of sewage going into the ocean are also concerned with this parasites' affect on sea life. Some areas do not allow flushable litter for this reason.

Cat feces is not the only place to contract the parasite. Anyone can get toxoplasmosis from infected, undercooked meat, particularly raw pork or lamb and raw unpasteurized milk, especially goat milk. Cats get the parasite from eating contaminated raw meat, mice, birds or soil. Cats fed raw food or cats allowed outside are more susceptible. Everyone should be careful feeding raw food and make sure it is handled with sanitary precautions to avoid toxoplasmosis, salmonella and *E.* coli infections.

If you feed raw food you should take extra precaution when cleaning the litter box. Cats can pass contaminated feces that could infect humans. Once a cat is infected with the toxoplasma organism, it stays in their bodies, rarely causing illness. It can not be eliminated with antibiotics. Most cats would test positive for exposure, so older cats are less likely to become newly infected. Daily cleaning of the litter box

reduces the likelihood of infection. You do not have to get rid of your cat just because you are pregnant and you do not have to be pregnant to get toxoplasmosis. Having someone else clean the litter box, or wearing gloves and washing your hands after cleaning greatly reduces the risk. Healthy adults can get toxoplasmosis also but are likely to only see flu-like symptoms.

It is recommended to replace plastic boxes every year, and to have one more **litter box** than you have cats, and if you have several levels in your home, you should have at least one on each floor. I have two litter boxes for my two cats but they choose to share, or pee

Laurie Nicholson of RocknRagz' Tiger
(seal mitted with blaze)

in one, and poop in the other. I have never tried a self-cleaning litter box but one day I would like to own the *Cat Genie,* if it is big enough for large cats.

Since Ragdolls are large cats you really need a larger than normal box. No cat wants to feel cramped. Gloie, from one of the Ragdoll Yahoo! groups uses storage type, *Rubbermaid* or *Sterlite* containers instead of the typical litter box for her Ragdoll Benji. I looked for these but had a hard time finding them without valleys and ridges in the bottom. There are litter boxes with one low side for easy entry and three high sides to keep litter and waste

Lynn Freeman's Nolte (blue bicolor)

Eve Kurpiers' Nuzzler (blue bicolor)

contained. If you have a cat that likes to back up to the edge to eliminate, this type may help keep more in the litter box. Some boxes are hooded and some have a rim that snaps on and angles in just a bit. There are special mats to contain litter scattered outside the box. Ragdolls can have longer hair on their britches and an occasional sanitary trim will help keep litter and litter box contents from clinging to that hair.

You need to have the **boxes located** in a private, quiet but not cramped area, where there is not high traffic, loud noises or a place your cat could feel trapped. Typically a cat will not eliminate where it eats, so don't keep the litter box close to the food area. The laundry room may seem like a good idea but the washer and dryer make unexpected sounds. It is recommended to place litter boxes in different areas of your house so your cat always feels like it can get to a box. Cats that don't like company may hesitate to walk through a room filled with people to get to their bathroom. If you have a dominant cat, it may intimidate other cats so that they don't want to pass the bully to get to a box. Giving cats multiple choices increases the likelihood they will feel comfortable and eliminate in a litter box.

I would say the number one unacceptable behavior is a cat not using the litter box.

Again, I would like to recommend Pam Bennett's book, *Think Like a Cat*. I have learned from her book and several websites that the first thing to do with a cat who is eliminating inappropriately is take it to the vet to out rule a health issue, as it could be associating pain with the box. See the chapter "No-No's— Deterring Unwanted Behavior."

Having a cat continue using the litter box, is easier than retraining it. One of the biggest reasons a cat will not use the litter box, other than a medical condition, is that the box is not clean enough. It could be that your cat may not like the location, privacy, size or shape of the litter box, litter choice, amount of litter in the box, or it could just be

Litter boxes that were slowly being moved to their permanent location accessed through the doggie-doors

and anxiety or a behavioral problem. Most cats seem to prefer about two inches of litter. It is recommended not to change litter or move the box to a new location abruptly.

A **soiled spot** needs to be completely cleaned, including the padding under the carpet. Simply washing rugs, beds or linens is often not enough to completely remove the odor. You may not be able to smell it after washing but if your cat can— it is more likely to be re-soiled. I have had *Prolsolve, Odorz Out, Urine Off, Oxiclean, Folex* and *Anti-Icky-Poo* recommended. I have only used *Nature's Miracle* enzyme cleaner because it claims to neutralize the odor. If a cat continues to eliminate in inappropriate areas that you know you have cleaned well with an enzyme based cleaner (not ammonia based) you can try covering the area with sticky tape, tinfoil, upside down carpet runners or placing a food bowl in that spot. After I clean an area that was soiled, I also mist the spot with pheromone spray.

I thought we had a grand set up for Skeamer's bathroom, so much so that we repeated it when we built our next home. We installed a doggie-door that went into an enclosed area in the garage, where we kept the litter box that we accessed from another larger door in the garage. It took a little training with all our cats initially to use the doggie-door. We start with the door installed in a cardboard box that they could get in and out of from other sides. We put food or treats in the box so when they went through the door they were rewarded. After they were no longer afraid to push the doggie-door open we moved the litter box inside the cardboard box. When we started they were kittens and had small enough litter boxes, so that this was not a problem. During this time the box was still open to allow access to the litter box without going through the doggie-door. As they learned what it was all about, we closed the sides of the cardboard box so they had to use the doggie-door. I added *Cat Attract* litter, as

an extra incentive for my cats to continue to use their boxes as I was slowly moving the whole ensemble a little at a time from the temporary bathroom location to where the doggie-door would permanently be installed.

We access the boxes by opening a latched door to the "litter rooms" from the garage. The cats get to them through the doggie-doors. Each cat has its own doggie-door and its own box. Our three "litter rooms" have been a framed plywood box with a hinged top, a section of a closet, and a base kitchen cabinet, depending on where it was going. All were larger than the litter box with plenty of standing room and two of the three have *Plexiglas* windows. Thankfully my husband is quite handy and has always been able to come up with something that works beautifully. I installed mats on the floor inside and outside the rooms to help catch litter. To help with odor control, I added a mesh type bag containing volcanic crystals.

I have recommended this setup many times until one of the people in a Yahoo! cat group saw her cat straining in the litter box with no output. Her cat turned out to have blockage. Had she not seen her cat struggling, it would have been longer before the problem was found. I am not able to see my cats in the litter box unless I go in to the garage and look through the windows in the access doors. I know now that I have to pay closer attention to the trips being made, and the amount of waste in the boxes. This would be true with any kind of covered or contained litter box.

Marsha Harris' Quincy (flame bicolor)

Sandy Baker's Rocky (seal lynx mitted)

No-No's—
Deterring Unwanted Behavior

Dollheaven Lexus of Kylador "Lexie"
(seal colorpoint)

Gloie Wall's Benji (flame point mitted lynx)

A loud "NO" or "ah-ah-ah" usually does the trick to deter unwanted behavior. You can also use a distraction, like a toy, a can filled with coins that make a loud noise when shaken, a squirt with water, or compressed air. I have also heard about people who hiss like a cat to let the cat doing something unwanted know its behavior is not approved of.

Whatever you choose to do, be consistent and make sure everyone in the house is on the same page with what is, and is not allowed. If you have one person allowing something and another saying "no," it is just going to create a misunderstanding.

Many behaviors natural to your cat, like scratching or scent marking are normal feline behaviors. Cats do not instinctively know that we may not want them to do certain things.

Remember to only use rewards and praise to train your cat. Any delayed scolding will just leave your cat confused and it may become fearful of you. Your cat may even want to retaliate. You should never hit, flick, shake, spank or punish your cat. Cats learn best by repeated praise, treats, or both. A treat can be petting, playing, or food rewards.

I know some people turn to **animal communicators** for help when an animal is not acting the way they want it to. I have never enlisted one, and remain skeptical of generalized predictions. A Certified Animal Behavior Consultant (**CABC**) may be able to shed light on a problem after observing your cat in your home. This is based on what I've read, not from experience. From what

Lynn Freeman's Dinky (seal bicolor)

I understand, a CABC comprehends cat's behavior and can often find the root cause of a problem. Once the cause is determined, steps can be made to fix the problem, not just sugarcoat the symptoms. Read more at iaabc.org, animalbehaviorsociety.org, or veterinarybehaviorists.org.

There are different kinds of feline **behavioral** issues from urine marking, separation anxiety, depression, or **obsessive compulsive** behaviors like over grooming. These can be caused by issues with new surroundings, a move, another cat in the home or yard, a new baby or new adult, company, noise fears (thunder, fireworks, car backfiring, bad weather), being groomed, given baths, and of course, visiting the vet.

Un-neutered male cats are known for **spraying**, but altered males and females can also spray. They may have seen another cat outside, or another cat's scent was brought into the house, and your cat wants to reestablish its territory. Spraying

and inappropriate elimination (eliminating outside the litter box) are two separate issues. Spraying is usually done on a vertical surface. Your cat will turn around, raise and wiggle its tail, spraying the vertical surface with urine that will be about the height of another cat's nose to establish territory. **Inappropriate elimination** of urine will leave a puddle or round spot on the floor or horizontal surface.

Owning a black light is helpful in checking for and finding soiled areas. I own a small black light. To use it I need the room very dark and must keep the light at a close distance from where I am checking to be able to see anything. I think the box should also have a warning that sock fuzz glows too, because before you know what all those glowing spots are, it can cause a bit of a panic.

Cats sometimes deposit feces in unusual places to claim territory. A cat peeing or pooping outside the litter box could be their way of telling you that you are not

Sandy Baker's Pippin (seal mitted with blaze)

Constance McCarthy's Nicodemus (seal colorpoint)

Mr. Tyler

Ms. Trinity

Karen Wright of Kylador
three week old kitten

Laurie Nicholson of
RocknRagz' Tia Maria

Marsha Harris' Quincy (flame bicolor)

keeping their box clean enough, or there is something they do not like about it. It could also be a behavioral or medical problem where they associate pain with using the litter box.

If herbal flower essences do not help behavioral issues in your cat, there are prescription drugs also, like: alprazolam (*Xanax*), amitriptyline (*Elavil*), buspirone (*Buspar*), clomipramine (*ClomiClam, Anafranil*), diazepam (*Valium*), fluoxetine (*Reconcile, Prozac*), and sertraline (*Zoloft*). I have never medicated a cat for behavioral issues but I know some people that are pleased with the results. Our cat Skeamer was given prednisone for itchy skin. Without a doubt, she saw things that were not there. We could see her watching invisible things move around. It was not worth the side effects it caused her, to stop her from scratching her skin, and we ended up using omega oils instead.

*E*very pet owner has things they will, or will not allow.

Thankfully, Ragdolls are not typically big climbers, probably due to their size and laid-back personality. I allow my cats almost everywhere except the kitchen counters, the tables we eat at, and my husband's bathroom sink. I know they do not always abide by my rules, but I consistently stick to what they can and cannot do, so there is no confusion. I prefer they stay out of our closet and baskets of warm, clean laundry fresh from the dryer. I would also appreciate it if they let me sleep the whole night through instead of walking all over me for a nightly petting.

I have tried in the evening before bedtime to play with my cats with an interactive toy, then put out more food, hoping they would sleep after playing and eating. Their

Tyler and Trinity in the clean clothes

Tyler and Trinity

Sandy Baker's Rocky (seal lynx mitted) and Pippin (seal mitted with blaze)

Trinity and Tyler

Marsha Harris' Quincy (flame bicolor)

Sandy Baker's Rocky (seal lynx mitted)

nocturnal nature seems to often override my efforts and sleep schedule. I have never rewarded the night time wake-up routines with feeding, but for the first few years of my cats' lives, being woken during the night was a regular occurrence. Thankfully, as my cats get older, my daytime efforts or my ability to sleep more soundly are paying off. Now it is rare when we are actually awakened during the night. Early mornings are still a problem. Cats are crepuscular, which means they are more active at dusk and dawn. I will not feed my cats before 7:30 am, but that does not stop them from letting me know morning has arrived the minute sunlight peaks in. My cats have their recommended cat perch by the window with a bird feeder outside to help keep their interest during the daytime, yet we often find them sound asleep facing the indoors.

If your cat jumping on **counters** or **furniture** is a problem you can make them less appealing. Try putting double-sided sticky tape on placemats set on the counters, or carpet protector runners, upside down with the nubby, anchor points facing up, or put pennies inside metal cans with lids, like coffee cans, on the counter, so that they tip and startle your cat when they jump up where they shouldn't be. For counter jumpers your first step should be to make sure no food or dirty dishes are left out to entice them.

There are several motion sensors that omit a spray of compressed air or make a sound when they detect motion. I bought the *TattleTale* sensor for our Christmas tree. I set it to sensitive, and if the tree was wiggled the alarm would go off. I don't mind my cats laying under the tree, or that I had to give up using ribbons and bows. I do mind them climbing the tree— both for their safety and for the sake of my sentimental ornaments. Even though my two are scared of sounds they hear daily, they soon got used to the *TattleTale* alarm, and would continue playing in the tree. We used to put the tree up

Marsha Harris' Tessie (seal point mitted)

Sandy Baker's Pippin (seal mitted with blaze)

Sandy Baker's Rocky (seal lynx mitted)

right after Thanksgiving but we now wait a little longer to keep life simpler. I hope to find a motion-activated ornament that plays a song to deter them. Some people put their tree in a playpen.

Plants can seem like play toys or a snack to some cats. I kept no houseplants and my hubby only sent me flowers at work, because Skeamer would eat anything. She even chewed on a cactus and used the sharp needles like floss, slowly pulling her teeth across them. Well, needless to say my plants were given away or went up to high places or hanging baskets out of reach, which makes them quite hard to water. As Skeamer got older and stopped jumping up on things, I slowly acquired plants again, and was finally able to enjoy a bouquet of flowers on my table.

When the kittens arrived, the plants had to go again. Of all the plants I had, only one was not poisonous. I have considered adding cat grasses in hopes that if my cats had their own greens to chew on, they would leave mine alone.

Some cats will not eat the plant, but will play in the dirt. If that is your only problem you can cover the dirt with a screen and put decorative rocks on top. Be sure to get large enough rocks that they are not a choking hazard. My best friend, Caroline, tried this with her cat, Angel. The rocks she added to her plants were large enough so that Angel left them alone but they need a fireplace screen to keep her from getting the rocks from the gas fireplace and batting them across the hardwood floor. I am sure my friend would like to quit hearing the rocks being played with at night, and stepping on them in the morning. You can try protecting your plants by spraying them with bitter apple deterrent, sprinkling them with pepper, or adding citrus fruit peels. Note that some citrus plants contain essential oils and should not be where your cat can consume it.

Most Ragdoll owners will tell you their Ragdoll rarely extends its claws on anything other than an allowable surface like a scratching post. For our furniture, I tried using the double-sided sticky tape on my sofa's corners that my cats were using as a scratching post, but all they did was move over two inches, and claw at a place without the tape. If your cat is scratching your furniture, simply say "no," show them their own scratching posts, and reward and praise your cat for using the approved surface.

To help encourage **scratching** on approved areas you should provide plenty of toys and different scratching surfaces, horizontal and vertical, cardboard or sisal. You can spray or sprinkle catnip on the post to make it more enticing. Cats typically like to stretch and scratch after waking from a catnap, so be sure to place them in areas where your cat sleeps. Trimming your cat's nails, using nail caps, double-sided sticky tape, deterrents, distraction or behavioral modification, are a few options.

Declawing is one subject that can draw heated debate. Some breeders have a statement in their contract that forbids declawing or having a tendonectomy done on your cat. Some people say that declawing will change your cat's personality, cause aggression or litter box issues— while others will disagree. Declawing is illegal in some European countries and considered inhumane or mutilation in others. It is not a decision to take lightly and you should discuss options with your vet and exhaust all other possible solutions first.

If you have tried everything, and you are to the point of relinquishing your pet to a shelter, making it stay outside, or euthanasia, you should talk to your vet. If you are going to declaw anyway, it is best to do it while the cat is young, but like any surgery, there are risks and pain. Older cats have a much harder time with the surgery and recovery. Discuss pain

Linda Dicmanis' Bingo (blue colorpoint) and Schniffley (seal colorpoint)

Marsha Harris' Quincy (flame bicolor)

Mary Becker's Tedrick "Teddy" (seal lynx mitted)

medication, risk and what to expect during recovery, with your vet.

A declaw or **onychectomy**, can be done with a scalpel but the newer laser method has a faster recovery time when done correctly. Make sure your vet is an experienced surgeon using the laser, because a laser used improperly can damage more tissue than the classic surgery. If the declaw is not done correctly, there is potential for the nail to regrow. It may cost a little more for the laser versus the classic declaw, but the laser beam typically seals off the nerve endings and has less bleeding and less post surgery pain. Either way, this operation is done under anesthesia and involves removing or amputation of the claw, along with the last bone of each toe. It will forever alter the way the cat naturally walks and will require the use of special litter for a while after the surgery.

Another surgical procedure that permanently renders a cat unable to claw is a **tendonectomy**. A ligament is cut on the underside of each toe, the claws remain, but they cannot be extended. With this procedure, it is extremely important that you trim the nails regularly to keep them from growing into your cat's foot pads, and causing pain or infection. Ragdolls should be indoor cats anyway, but if you do any of these procedures it is even more important that your cat be kept indoors— as it can no longer climb a tree and is at a big disadvantage in defending itself.

When my two sweet cats act out their sibling rivalries, I usually try to distract them with a toy or a loud sound. I may not always know the reason the squabble started. It could have been that one of my cats saw a stray outside and misdirected its aggression on the only cat it could get to. One cat may not feel well, or may want to be alone and the other cat intrudes on its space. Our cats test each other to see how much they can get away with from the

Karen Wilkinson's Merlin (seal point mitted) and Myst (blue colorpoint)

Shirley Stubrich's Rajah (blue colorpoint)

Susan Thompson's Dollheaven Tallulah (blue bicolor) and Dollheaven Tinkerbell (blue torbie point mitted)

Shirley Stubrich's Marley (blue bicolor)

Gloie Wall's Benji (flame point mitted lynx)

Linda Dicmanis' Schniffley (seal colorpoint)

other; whose spot, whose toy, who is getting petted more; along with vying for the alpha cat position in our two cat hierarchy.

In some animals there is a link between **aggression** and feeding schedule. Since we free-feed after breakfast I assumed that was not an issue until I started watching for it. Even if they still have dry food left in their bowls but wanted their morning wet food, or if Tyler didn't like his particular flavor, he would be more aggressive toward Trinity. It took me paying closer attention, to see that most of the time he acted out more in the morning. Some animals that are fed at set times can show aggression about an hour before meal time, as hunger or frustration can lead to aggression. If you have a cat showing aggression before meal time, simply serving smaller meals more often or free-feeding may help. You can also try filling treat balls with regular dry kibble for your cat to have to work for its food during the day.

I use various feline pheromone plug-ins or pheromone sprays to calm my cats and have tried *Bach's Rescue Remedy* and *Feliway*. I can't say for sure if they worked, but I don't know that they didn't work either. A lot of people feel they are very effective. Just don't put them near the litter box. I mist pheromone spray on "accident" spots after they are thoroughly cleaned.

There are several flower essence remedies for aggression like tiger lily, vine, beech, or holly. For the submissive cat, heather, rock rose, centaury, and larch are recommended. Flower essences are generally liquid you administer by putting in your cat's mouth, adding to their water, rubbing on the inside of their ears, pads of their paws, or nose. Some of the older flower remedies contained alcohol. The newer versions are alcohol-free combinations of several flower remedies. Some flower remedies in pastille form like candy, pill, or lozenges, intended for human use contains xylitol,

Gloie Wall's Katie (seal colorpoint)

Gloie Wall's Benji (flame point mitted lynx)

which is harmful to pets— so read the label. We have some issues with Tyler being aggressive toward his sister, other than just at breakfast. Having them altered usually reduces this behavior, but Tyler will still nip at Trinity's heels or attack and pin her down. She tries to get away or hisses in an attempt to get him to leave her alone. The water bottle never seems to be near me at the right time to spray him for his mean behavior, and my hope that Trinity will give him some of his own medicine in return— never seems to happen.

When Tyler is being aggressive I have started putting a new collar with a bell on him. He doesn't like it and it diverts his attention from his sister. This seems to help, at least for a short time. After the squabble ends, I take the collar off so he doesn't get used to it. I hesitate to put him on some kind of kitty *Prozac*, but I do not want to go to meds until I have exhausted all other avenues. It is a good thing his little sister is smarter, more coordinated, and quicker than her big brother. Remember never try to break up a cat fight with your hands.

No cat owner wants to be **bitten** or played with too rough either. Our first beautiful cat, Skeamer was part feral. We got her young as a single cat and we met almost every criteria for having a biting cat. We could not change the fact that her father was a feral cat, but if we had left her with her siblings longer, they, along with the mother cat, would have taught her that biting hard would not be tolerated. We also played with our hands— a big no-no, but we didn't know better at the time. We should have used toys to play with her and redirected her to a toy or stopped all interaction with her when she bit.

If appropriate rules are not set at kitten stage, your cat may think hands, feet and ankles are play toys. After having a singleton and then a sibling pair, I think that your cat having another to play with helps with misplaced aggression, because they can play rough with each other, and you can bet one will let the other know when they were bitten too hard. We also had good results with becoming the alpha when we were bitten. Instead of the normal reaction of pulling away when she bit us, we would push our arm, hand or whatever she was biting farther into her mouth. This was uncomfortable to her, and it did not trigger the hunter reflex like when we withdrew, making her instinctively follow.

After we lost Skeamer, I learned that cats can have **petting induced aggression**. It is known by other names, rolling skin syndrome and feline hyperesthesia syndrome, but they all simply mean that petting can only be done for short periods of time because the cat is either very sensitive, or may be feeling pain from being petted, which causes the aggression. Skeamer's back would often twitch or ripple after we petted her, like we made her skin crawl– which was another symptom. I wish during her life we had known about this obsessive compulsive

My Skeamer
(DLH, domestic longhair)

disorder. We may have tried to treat it, but at the very least we would have had a reason for her sudden aggressive behavior.

We learned late in Skeamer's life the things we should have done differently and I went overboard with Tyler and Trinity because I didn't want to be bitten anymore. When we got Tyler and Trinity we ONLY played with toys. If they bit, we sternly said "NO BITE," and stopped playing with them. Both will occasionally nibble, but it is never aggressive or hateful. Some people call these love bites. Sometimes when I am trying to sleep Trinity will carefully grasp the skin on my

knuckle with her teeth, and pull up on my hand as if to say "lift your hand and pet me."

Ragdolls are not overly **talkative** cats; however, they will soon learn that if you reinforce unwanted meowing, by giving your cat attention or food when they meow, that it worked to get them what they wanted. Tyler has learned that if he comes to me and meows, I will pick him up. He trained me well. Tyler and Trinity must see "softie" written on my forehead and will tell me when they want to be picked up, played with, or fed. Trinity will cry like she is dying during a bath or in the carrier on the way to the vet. If Tyler is crying, Trinity will go check to see if he is okay. Even if Tyler is being mean to his sister, she will still mother him, unless he is crying during a bath— then I guess she figures he is on his own. Thankfully they don't meow too often or loudly. It took me a little while, but most of the time I can tell who is talking and what each meow or sound means.

Gloie Wall's Katie (seal colorpoint) and
Benji (flame point mitted lynx)

Sandy Baker's Pippin (seal mitted with blaze)

Your Ragdoll and Travel

Kylador As You Like It "Basil" (blue bicolor) with Presley, a Nova Scotia Duck Tolling Retriever

Bridlepath Mercedes of Kylador "Sadie" (seal bicolor)

Karen Wright of Kylador's two kittens (seal colorpoint and seal mitted)

I am a cat person but I will say that most dog owners have the upper-hand when it comes to taking vacations. With doggie daycare and boarding kennels, your dog is likely to have a grand time while you are away. There are feline **boarding** facilities also but most cats do not do as well being outside their home, unless they are accustomed to the secondary home, and the person watching them. I have heard of cat owners who can simply pack up their cat, and take it to stay with family or friends and the cat is comfortable with the temporary surroundings.

When Skeamer was diagnosed with kidney failure I was still self-employed. If I wasn't there, the store was not open, but I wanted to know how she was doing. I had read about what signs to watch for as her kidneys declined, and I did not want her suffering at home while I was at work clueless to her needs. I bought peace of mind when I bought nine netcams and a program where I could watch all the cameras from work on the computer. With her being older, she was usually in one of the cameras range sleeping. I found it comforting to know she was not in distress.

I didn't need the netcams with Tyler and Trinity, but since I had them already, it was nice to check and see what mischief they were up to. As kittens they would sometimes go for hours and not show up in any of the cameras, but I soon learned they were just napping the day away out of the netcams view.

Netcams are great for monitoring your pet's eating, litter box use, or for behavior that seems to only happen in your absence. There is even a way to record movement and email the video to yourself, but it is one quick way to become the "crazy cat lady." One of my sales reps could

All nine photos are from Ragdoll breeder, Karen Wright of Kylador

not believe I had nine "kitty cams" as she called them, but thought they were a great idea. Netcams are now advertised for these uses.

Since I no longer have a retail business, I quit using them. The last time we went away I dragged them out and thought I had three of the nine working. I could hardly wait to check on my furbabies when we got to a secure wireless connection. I was disappointed that I had only set one camera correctly. They are not the easiest things to configure. My sister-in-law, Debbie, was cat sitting, and we talked everyday, which is reassuring— but I still like being able to see my babies. She let me know that Trinity was holding out for me to come home, but Tyler just accepted the new food giver and wanted belly rubs from her. Little traitor... now if he would have given her that beloved head tilt, that I think is reserved just for me, I would have been quite jealous.

My husband and I put off vacations for years because Skeamer needed daily medication,

and it seemed too much to ask someone to give her medication. When we had to be away we had friends or family come to our home every day— preferably twice a day.

Having someone come to your home, so that your cats can keep life as close to normal, is usually your best bet. It is a good idea to have **instructions** describing how and what to feed, medicines to give and how to give them, your vet info including location and after hours emergency phone numbers, where you keep the carriers, and what to do or who to call if they can't make it by your home. You may also want to let your vet know who is caring for your cat in your absence, and give instructions for emergencies, especially if there is a chance you can't be reached by phone.

When we are going to be away, I use the pheromone plug-in *Comfort Zone*, to help with any **separation anxiety** and I put a few articles of clothing that I have worn where my cats like to nap. I call home and talk on our answering machine to our cats

Laurie Nicholson of RocknRagz
blue colorpoint kitten

Gloie Wall's Benji (flame point mitted lynx)

so they can hear me, and I plan to get a new little toy ball that records my voice and plays it back when our cats touch it. I put dry cat food in treat balls to give them something to play with and occupy their time, and ask the sitter to do the same. A treat ball is made of hard plastic with a small hole you put treats in; as your cat rolls it around, they fall out.

My pet sitters have always been family or friends so I do not have to worry, but I hate leaving my cats and tear-up every time. I am sure I miss them more than they miss me. The first time my husband had cat duty they did not let him sleep. When I returned, Trinity, who is usually the less needy of my two, had to be right with me. Tyler pouted and let me know that he was not pleased with my absence by acting like he could care less that I returned. He would forget he was pouting and want to be cuddled, then remember he was mad, and walk away, tuck his front legs under and just stare at me. After a few days, and after the suitcases were put away, life went back to normal.

If I ever have to be away and I cannot find someone I know to watch my cats, I would ask my vet, friends and fellow cat owners for recommendations. I would want the **pet sitter** to be trustworthy and responsible. I would want to know what they do in case of bad weather, an emergency, or if they could not get to my home. I would not want them coming to my home after attending to another home with sick or diseased animals, as some diseases can be spread by contact, on shoes, clothing, or hands. Well before my trip I would want them to come to my home to see how they act with my pets, and how my pets respond to them. I would want to be comfortable leaving my home and pets with them, and know that I clearly understood what their services included. Check references, and find out if they are certified, bonded or insured.

Some cat owners prefer to travel with their pets. I would want my cats to be current on all vaccinations, and flea control. I would take along most things I would have in my emergency and first aid kits. See the chapter "Dangers and Emergencies." With all pet travel I would want my cats wearing a GPS collar, or at least a collar or harness with an identification tag. There is always the potential to become separated from your cat; that your cat could be lost, or escape its carrier.

When traveling with your cats **in the car**, you should use the seatbelt on your carrier, kennel, or crate, even for short trips. Your cat should not be loose in the car while you are driving as it could get under the pedals. If you are in an accident your cat could be thrown from the car, injured, or get loose when the doors are opened. If you do not have a large enough kennel or crate so your cat can move around, you should stop occasionally, lock the doors with yourself and the cat inside the car. Then you can safely let your cat out of the carrier to use the litter box, move around, play a little, eat or drink (if their stomach handles car rides okay), then return it to the carrier before any car doors are opened. Some cats prefer to see you, and some will cry less if turned away from you. Each cat is different. Skeamer was completely quiet. Tyler does not make much noise in the car but Trinity sounds like she is suffering terribly with her long, loud almost constant cries.

For short car trips, especially those to the veterinarians, I spray a calming pheromone spray in the carriers about ten minutes before I put the cats in them. I do not include toys for a short trip, but if you are planning a longer trip with your cat, having toys, blankets or beds they are familiar with can help ease anxiety.

If you don't know how your cat responds to traveling, it is a good idea to feed smaller amounts or withhold food a little while before the trip to reduce stomach upset. If you are not driving your own car you should check with your rental car companies, airlines, railways or other mode of travel to find out what their rules are regarding pets. There are

Kylador As You Like It "Basil" (blue bicolor) relaxing on the carrier

Gloie Wall's Katie (seal colorpoint) sporting a collar

Sandy Baker's Rocky (seal lynx mitted) on a leash

airlines that solely fly pets. Some airlines do not allow pets to travel with you in the cabin and put them in the cargo area, and some do not allow pets at all. There are often firm rules as to the carrier size, and where it must be placed during flights. With all airline travel If you feel more comfortable you can enlist the help of a travel agent, or pet shipper. Visit ipata.com, PetFlight.com, HappyTailsTravel.com, or the Independent Pet and Animal Transportation Association International Inc. Some cats can benefit from prescription medication to stay calm during stressful events like travel. Be sure to tell your vet if your cat will be traveling on an airline, as altitude is thought to alter its response to some medicine.

Kiwimagic New Zealand Pride "Pascal" of Guysndolls (blue point)

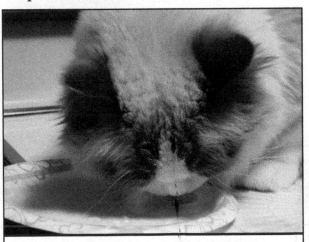

Eve Kurpiers' Nuzzler (blue bicolor)

Gloie Wall's Benji (flame point mitted lynx)

Before your trip, it is a good idea to find **pet friendly** hotels. Make sure "pet" includes cats and not just dogs. One pet friendly hotel, The *Algonquin* in New York City even has a resident feline who just happens to be a Ragdoll named Matilda.

In **hotels** I would use the "do not disturb" sign, to keep a maid from opening the door and possibly letting my cats out. When you are not in the room your cat should be in its large kennel, crate, carrier, pop-up tent, or the hotel bathroom that you have cat-proofed ahead of time. See the chapter "Dangers and Emergencies." It may be hard to get a cat to come out from under a hotel bed, and I seriously doubt they get vacuumed and cleaned under on a regular basis.

Karen Wright of Kylador's Watson

Kylador As You Like It "Basil" (blue bicolor)

Feline Traits and Characteristics

A cat's **eyesight** is superior to ours in low light conditions and for sensing movement. For outdoor cats this is a necessity for nocturnal hunting. The retina contains two types of receptors, rods and cones. Cones detect color and rods detect light and movement. Humans have more cones, and we are better equipped to detect colors. It is believed that cats can see black, white, shades of gray, blue, yellow and green. Cats have more rods, and that is what helps them detect movement, like prey, and see better in low light. They also have a greater field of vision than humans, especially peripheral vision. I would argue this when I am trying to get my cats' attention— apparently they can see me, they just choose to ignore me. Felines see the sharpest at two to three feet and can more easily detect movement than stationary objects. The cat's eye also has a special membrane or layer of cells called the tapetum lucidum that acts like a mirror in affect bouncing light back through the retina. This is what gives cats' eyes that glow at night, and allows them to see more in low light than humans or even dogs. Unlike humans, cats have a third eyelid to keep the eye from getting dry and to protect it from damage, dirt, and debris. The **third eyelid** is also called a nictitating membrane or palpebra tertia. I have watched my vet press on my cats' eyes to check the health of their third eyelid. It is on the inside corner of a cat's eye and is not often noticed on a healthy cat. This third eyelid can sometimes be seen if your cat is happy or sleeping (see the inset photo bottom left). If your cat's third eyelid looks differently than it normally does, you should take your cat to the vet.

Most cats' eyes glow green, or yellow in photos. Ragdolls beautiful blue eyes typically show up red in photos because cats with blue eyes often lack melanin pigment. I have found to avoid red-eye in photos with my point and shoot camera that I have to be in a well-lit room, and not use the flash or red-eye setting. With the flash off I need a steady hand, steady shutter finger, and the camera set to a fast

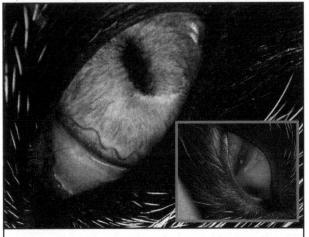

Close up of Tyler's eye and third eyelid (inset)

Karen Wilkinson's Ragdolls Myst (blue colorpoint) and Merlin (seal point mitted)

shutter speed to avoid blurry photos. Any movement from me or the subject causes blur. My cats are seldom stationary unless they are sleeping. I prefer to get the shot before it is over and do touch up with photo editing software. Before I started turning the flash off, Ms. Trinity learned that when I pointed my camera at her it was going to hurt her eyes, and she would squint before the flash ever fired. Using a camera that has a bounce or diffused flash that can be pointed somewhere other than your cat's eyes should also help.

A cat can detect higher pitched sounds than humans or dogs. If you have ever

recessive and dominant genes that are so far out of my understanding I will not attempt to go into detail. From the little I think I understand, the gene for being all white and the gene for blue eyes are two separate factors but are in close proximity to each other. When one gene is passed to offspring, the genes in close proximity are passed on also. This is called the Waardenburg syndrome. Even odd-eyed, solid white cats are more likely to be deaf on the side with the blue eye.

A deaf cat only has a minor disability if kept indoors and you learn not to startle it. A cat that is at a disadvantage in one of their

Mary Becker's Toulouse "Touie"
(blue point mitted with small blaze)

Patricia Besaw's Bellapalazzo
Maximillion (BEW, blue-eyed white)

seen a cat make a silent meow, more than likely it did meow, just at a pitch too high for your ear to hear. Our **hearing** is similar to cats at the low range but they can detect higher pitched frequencies than we can, and pinpoint the sound location faster and more accurately. Don't believe me? Just try to open that tuna can without your cat running in from another room. A cat has 32 individual muscles in each ear and can move each ear independently of the other as well as move its body in one direction with its ears pointing in another.

Often you will find more blue-eyed, solid white cats to be **deaf** due to genetics of

senses will learn to make the most of the other senses it does have. A deaf cat may meow louder than other cats simply because it cannot hear how loud it is meowing. A deaf cat will likely sense the vibrations you make when you walk. If your deaf cat is not sleeping, you can try to make sure it sees you before you pet it. It is even possible to teach some cats a form of sign language. These signs can be whatever you and your cat come up with. For example showing the cat its bowl or the food bag could signal meal time, while something as simple as patting your leg could mean to "come here." The Ragdoll breed standard is for blue eyes. They are typically colorpoint, bicolor, mitted or van pattern instead of solid white and are no more likely to be deaf than other cats. I have heard that there is no such thing as a solid white Ragdoll, that the white simply masks the other colors, unless of course you are talking about a true albino.

A domestic cat's **sense of smell** is up to 14 times stronger than our own. Cats can also smell with the roof of their mouth, well sort of, cats have a vomeronasal or Jacobson's organ. We find ourselves telling our cats "your mouth is open" after they smell something and get this funny expression with their mouth slightly gapping, called the flehmen reaction. Cats

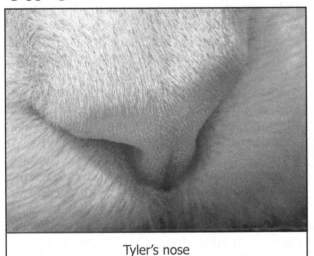
Tyler's nose

actually pick up the smell on their tongue, and then touch their tongue to the roof of their mouth, where there are a bundle of olfactory nerves just above their palate.

Cats often **mark** their scents on what they feel is theirs, or in greeting. The greeting you get with their tail up, or when they rub their face on you or knead you, are all ways they transfer their scent. They have scent glands in those areas, and they are just releasing their scent on to an object or human they like. A cat spraying is one of the least desirable forms of marking to pet owners, but it is the cat's way of saying "this is mine."

My cats all kneaded a spot before laying down, whether it was me, a blanket or bed. Each of my cats kneaded very differently. Some **knead** with only a few flicks of the end of one paw then the other, and some march in place for minutes at a time. I find it endearing as long as it does not go on so long as to start making a sensitive spot on me. Some people call this "making biscuits." Un-spayed females may knead more just before they go into heat. Newborn kittens knead their mother's belly when suckling. I have seen a shirt with "my cat kneads me" written on it that I thought was cute.

As mentioned earlier in the chapter

Kylador Canadian Chloe (blue bicolor)
with two kittens

"Grooming and Cleaning," a cat's tongue has papillae, hair-like backward facing projections make of keratin. Keratin is what our hair and nails are made of. The sandpaper feel when your cat licks you, is what helps them in grooming. A cat's tongue can sense flavor, texture and temperature. A cat can reduce its body temperature by panting. Cats have fewer **taste** buds than humans do, but this does not keep my cats from being quite selective about what they will eat. Most cats prefer food at room temperature but I know a few who like ice in their water. A mother cat uses her tongue to lick her kittens' genitals to urge them to urinate or defecate.

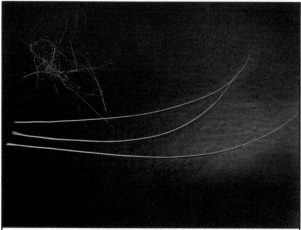

Three whiskers I found on the floor. I placed them next to cat hair to show the size difference

Gloie Wall's Benji (flame point mitted lynx)

Whiskers aid your cat by helping them sense the size of any opening, and in determining distances, sizes, shapes, and with balance. Cats use their whiskers as receptors to feel vibrations and locate things. Your cat may lose a whisker now and then. You can tell by the thickness that it is not an ordinary hair when you find one. Never cut your cat's whiskers. It could be uncomfortable if not downright painful— not to mention it could take months for a new set to grow. Whisker roots are up to three times deeper than normal cat hair and contain blood sinuses that connect to nerve bundles, and are sensitive to pressure; even a light touch can cause your cat to blink.

Cats are diphyodont, meaning they have two sets of **teeth**; deciduous or baby teeth and permanent. They have four types of teeth, the incisors used for picking things up and for grooming, the canines or fangs for holding prey and tearing, and the premolars and molars used for breaking-up food, and for carrying or holding something in their mouth. Kittens are born without teeth. At three or four weeks old the baby teeth start coming in and by six weeks all 26 are there. When they are four or five months old the baby teeth fall out and are replaced with their 30 permanent teeth. Cats have 12 less teeth than adult dogs. This change happens often without you knowing it. I happened to see blood on Tyler's ruff and started looking

Marsha Harris' Tessie (seal point mitted)

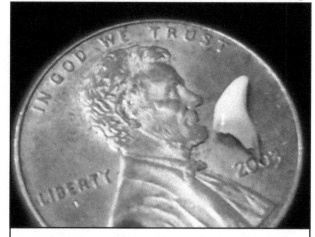

Trinity's baby tooth that I found in Tyler's ruff

Sandy Baker's Pippin (seal mitted with blaze)

Shirley Stubrich's Marley
from Kylador (blue bicolor)

him over. I found a bloody tooth, but his mouth looked fine. When I inspected Trinity, I found that it was her tooth that she had lost in his fur. I know they lost more than that one, but it was the only one I found.

A cat's **ears** provide a clue to its mood, just like its vocalization, tail, head, whiskers, and eyes. Ears forward and upright is usually an indicator of a content or happy cat; ears lain back, you better watch out— your cat is mad or scared. A tail twitching typically is a sign of aggression, while an upright tail often signals contentment.

Tyler is known for greeting those he likes with his **tail** held high, followed by a leg

rub, and an invitation to smell his anal glands. It is his way of saying, "Hello, glad to see you, I think you're alright." Out of all cat species, domestic cats are the ones that can hold their tail upright while walking. Tyler and Trinity often walk with their tails up, while Skeamer almost always had hers down. Each cat is unique but after a short time you will soon learn the language of your cat, and what your cat is saying, by its body language and sounds.

Cats can make more **vocal sounds** than dogs, some say over a hundred. No doubt you will soon discern the difference between a long or short meow, chirp, meep and trill. I love the sound of a cat purring,

Shalane Doucette's RW SGC BoysnRags Maximus
"Max" of PalaceCats (blue bicolor)

Sandy Baker's Pippin (seal mitted with blaze)

which is often a sign of contentment. Cats will also purr when stressed or near death. Purring is thought to have a calming and healing effect. A mother cat will purr, chirp and give soft meows to her kittens for them to locate her for milk, and offer them comfort, and security.

Trinity chatters at the birds, hisses at her brother, and does a demanding loud meow when she wants us awake. Tyler meeps when he wants to be picked up, and when he is excited because breakfast is to be served. It took a little while, but most of the time I can tell which cat is talking without seeing it, and more often than not, know what is happening that is causing it, or what they want. The one I do not understand is when both of my cats will cry when they carry small soft toys around. We have renamed those toys "cry-n-carry" toys. I don't know if they are saying "look at me" or think of it as a kitten, or captured prey they want to give us, but we hear the cries long before they round the corner with the toy in their mouth. I have heard of other Ragdolls doing this, but this one stumps me as to what I am supposed to do with the toy covered in saliva dropped at my feet.

Felines have a **righting reflex** and great sense of equilibrium that comes from their inner ear. This is why a cat often lands on their feet from a fall. They need enough height, typically about three feet, which gives them time to get their legs facing downward; but not so much height their bodies simply take too hard of a hit. The cat first starts by turning its head, then down their flexible spine the body follows, with the hind quarters rotating last. Cats can fall asleep and fall or get distracted and lose their footing. Cats' claws are usually able to grab on, if the surface allows, and keep it from falling. I have seen my cats fall asleep and fall off of what they were laying on. Thankfully it was never high enough to cause injury. They look embarrassed, and have shot me a look of disdain like I caused the incident.

Trinity watching a squirrel

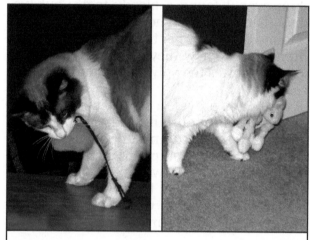

Tyler and Trinity with their "cry-n-carry" soft toys

Constance McCarthy's Ezekiel (seal point mitted)

Gloie Wall's Benji (flame point mitted lynx)

Karen Wright of Kylador's two bicolor Ragdolls

If your cat has fallen from a high object or does not act normal after a fall, a trip to the vet to check for internal injuries or broken bones is a must. Injuries sustained from a cat falling from greater than two stories is referred to as high-rise syndrome.

One of the reasons that cats can bend in contortionist shapes is that they have more vertebrae than humans. Cats have over 200 bones and over 500 muscles and are typically very coordinated. I have heard people say their Ragdoll is clumsy, while others think they have the same grace as other breeds. A cat's rear feet often land where their front feet were, and oddly enough they are one of the few animals that step with both right feet, and then both left feet. Cats are digitigrades which means they walk on their toes and their claws are protractable. It always amazes me to watch a cat delicately walk around things sitting on a shelf without knocking them over— unless of course it was on purpose to get attention.

In addition to the extraordinary uses of their senses, cats also have an uncanny ability that acts like a compass. There are cases of cats traveling for miles to get back to their homes. Some cats can detect the energy of a thunderstorm, or earthquake, sense when a seizure is about to strike their human companion, or when someone is about to die. Some cats have been known to wake their owners during a fire or be incredibly adept at sensing when their owners are in danger. Cats have also been said to be great at discerning someone's personality.

I do not know how much predicting my cats could do. I would bet they would be under the bed in any case of real or perceived danger, leaving me to fend for myself. I do know that my cats know when my husband or I are sick, and it seems they know when I am sad. I have heard we release certain endorphins that a cat can sense. One night when I was sick and had gone to bed early I woke to find the floor by my side of the bed, covered with all their soft toys which they had carried in during the night. Another time when my husband was injured they seldom left his side.

Many people can attest to the fact that their cat will go to the one non-cat person in the room. I have always wondered why that is. Some speculate that it has to do with eye contact. The cat lovers in the room are the most likely to be looking at the cat, making eye contact. The person who prefers the cat not come to them, is probably not looking or making eye contact with the cat. In cat language, not making eye contact is a nonthreatening gesture so the cat goes to the least threatening person.

Cats can have three different **blood types**, type *A*, *B*, and very rarely *AB*. As with people, the blood group must be matched or the cats' antibodies will destroy the alien blood cells. Unlike with people there is no universal blood type *O* in cats. The most common blood type is *A*, but there is a small chance, less than ten percent, that a Ragdoll will have blood type *B*. In purebreds, certain breeds show different frequency of having type *B* blood. Some breeds have been found to have no type *B*, while others can be as high as 50%.With non-pedigree cats the blood type varies greatly with geographic location. The most severe reaction is usually when type *B* is given to a cat with type *A* blood.

Cats can have something similar to the RH negative factor found in humans, where even if given the same blood type, they can have a transfusion reaction. In cats, this red cell antigen was identified as Mik. You can read more about this at interscience. wiley.com/journal/120715435/abstract.

Blood group incompatibility can cause a severe reaction or even death if a cat is given the wrong blood type during a transfusion or even from a mother cat to her own kitten. This is often diagnosed as fading kitten syndrome, neonatal isoerythrolysis, or haemolysis of the newborn. The queen transfers antibodies through her colostrum or first milk along with antibodies generated from vaccines, exposure to proteins or infections and antibodies to the "wrong" blood type. A kitten with incompatible blood type should avoid suckling within the first 24 to 48 hours after birth when the colostrum antibodies will absorb in the kittens intestines. Depending on how different the antibodies are, how much colostrum is suckled in the first few days and the amount of antibodies the kitten's intestines absorb, all affect the symptoms. Those affected will often fade or become weak and pale. They may have red colored urine, anemia,

Nenes Rags Miley (seal lynx point) of PalaceCats with kittens only hours old

Karen Wright of Kylador's Leif and Autumn

Sandy Baker's Pippin (seal mitted with blaze)

become jaundiced or die suddenly with no symptoms. If this is caught early enough steps can be taken to try to save the kitten but often it is discovered too late. I am aware that most of you reading this will be getting your Ragdoll already altered from a breeder when it is allowed to go to its new home around 12 weeks old and this will not pertain to you. I just found it interesting enough to share.

We always joked that with a kitten it was either on or off, and that somewhere there must be a switch. Cats sleep a lot. Adult cats can sleep up to eighteen hours a day and by nature are nocturnal creatures.

Most cat lovers know this from long ago, but it has now been proven that petting a cat can reduce a person's stress, depression, and blood pressure. Pets provide wonderful companionship, and offer affection. An adult that loved a pet as a child is thought to be more compassionate to animals and people as an adult. The cat also receives enjoyment from the time and attention they get from you— playing, petting, grooming, cuddling and simply loving them. Cats are even being used as emotional assistance animals in nursing homes or with veterans suffering from post traumatic stress disorders.

Sonja Phillips' Tucker Bee (seal point mitted)

Sandy Baker's Rocky (seal lynx mitted)

Marsha Harris' Quincy (flame bicolor)

Constance McCarthy's Nicodemus
(seal colorpoint)

Veterinarians and Vaccinations

Choosing a veterinarian is hard work. I live in a small town and I am on my fourth vet. Dogs seem to have the upper hand in receiving health care over cats. Dogs are taken to the vet more, adopted more, and are relinquished to shelters less often than cats.

The less frequent visits to the vet could be caused by cats' ability to hide pain or illness. I wanted to find a qualified vet that cherishes cats as much as I do, that stays up-to-date on the current medical information, handles my cat like they would their own, that is open minded enough for me to discuss information

at the clinic, if they have an in-house lab or pharmacy, the hours, number of veterinarians at the practice, who handles emergencies, and emergency hours, if they offer boarding and how close they are to my home— all play a part in my choice.

The American Animal Hospital Association (AAHA) membership signifies that a veterinary professional has voluntarily pursued, and met AAHA's standards. To be **board-certified** in a particular area of veterinary medicine the veterinarian has to have studied an additional two to four years

Karen Wright of Kylador's Ragdolls and dog

Karen Wright of Kylador's Ragdoll kitten on a scale

I gather in my own research or from talking with another vet. It is also important to me, to be with my pet at all times during the appointment. I do not want my cat being taken to other rooms that I cannot go with them for blood draws or procedures.

To find a **new vet**, I ask other pet owners for recommendations. I want to know their qualifications, their ability to do specialty procedures, and what diagnostic tests they can do at the clinic. Finding out if x-rays, MRI or CT scans are offered on-site, what treatments and surgeries they perform

in a **specialty area** and passed a rigorous exam. Veterinarian specialties can include: cardiology, ophthalmology, dermatology, dentistry, radiology, neurology, orthopedics, reproduction, nutrition, internal medicine or behavior. You can find a cat specialist at catvets.com/findadoctor/findadoctor.aspx, or myveterinarian.com. If you have a disability, are elderly, or lack transportation, there are mobile clinics in some areas that can come to your home.

If integrating or being knowledgeable on alternative medicine, holistic, homeopathic or complementary therapy like acupuncture or feline chiropractic is important to you, now is the time to find if your veterinarian's views match your own. Find out if they are against it, or if they will use it instead, or in addition to traditional medicine. Alternative medicines and supplements are not regulated like traditional medicines, even for human consumption— so you can be sure that the regulations for safe use for our pets trail even further behind. You can find a veterinarian who practices holistically at ahvma.org. Acupuncture should not cause stress to your cat and it is not without risk. You can read more at ivas.org and aava.org.

There are a few websites that you may find helpful if you are interested in **herbal medicine** like the American Botanical Council herbalgram.org, National Animal Supplement council at nasc.cc, Veterinary Botanical Medical at vbma.org, and Herb Research at herbs.org.

Marsha Harris' Quincy (flame bicolor) and Tess (seal mitted colorpoint)

It is helpful if your vet is familiar with the Ragdoll breed. Ragdoll kittens tend to gain about a pound per month until they are a year old. I hear time and time again, of Ragdoll owners being told their cat is overweight by vets who are not familiar with the breed. Ragdolls should not be fat cats, and I am not saying there are not overweight Ragdolls— just that they are a large, heavy breed. The breed standard even says they may have a fat pad on their lower abdomen. An active cat is less likely to be overweight, and they will surely enjoy the interactive play time with you.

I do not want to use an **emergency clinic** as a standard vet or wait until an emergency to choose one. I feel knowing where the closest emergency clinic is located, and their hours should be researched. I visited some of the local veterinarian clinics without my cats, just to meet them, talk with them and the staff, and see the clinic and its cleanliness. I know I go to the extreme but I want to know that the examination room

Marsha Harris' Quincy (flame bicolor) and Tess (seal mitted colorpoint)

LionsRoyale Royal William of RocknRagz
(cream colorpoint)

Bridlepath Mercedes of Kylador "Sadie"
(seal bicolor)

has been cleaned and disinfected before I take my cat out of the carrier and set it onto the examining table, or scale. So I ask. I have not taken my own sanitary wipes or towels to put over the examining table... yet. They probably think I am crazy. My concern about germs and disease is the same in hospitals where I use hand sanitizer. When a pet is sick, it is often taken to the vet and I do not want my cats to get some contagious disease from the clinic, fleas or flea eggs, from the pets that were there before mine. If the waiting room is full of barking dogs or other cats, and it is going to be a while before we can be seen, I give them my cell number and we wait in the car until they are ready for us. Remember to never leave your pet unattended in the vehicle, especially when it is cold or hot outside.

Cats are living longer today than ever before. The old saying that a **cat-year** is equal to seven human years is not quite right. Cats age faster in their early years, and can reproduce as a kitten at just six months old. A junior cat, seven months through two years old is equal to a person in their late teens or early twenties. A three to six year old is equal to about a thirty to forty year old person, while a seven to ten year old cat is considered mature. Eleven to fourteen years is considered senior and fifteen and over is considered geriatric. Most veterinarians recommend food changes and annual blood work begin around age seven. Some vets now have hospice care available, which is a nice feature to offer in my opinion.

We will probably continue to see more cats living in to their geriatric years. This is due to more people keeping their cat indoors, giving their cats proper care, exercise, nutrition, regular veterinarian visits, and dental care. Skeamer's elevated kidney levels were found during routine blood work before a dental cleaning. She showed no symptoms. Knowing early let us change her diet to a prescription formula food.

Gloie Wall's Benji (flame point mitted lynx)

Kylador Canadian Chloe (blue bicolor)

You should always take your cat to the vet in a carrier and keep your cat in the carrier instead of loose inside of the automobile, for your safety and your pets. See the chapter "Your Cat and Travel" earlier in the book.

Ragdolls will need a larger **carrier** than most cats. I tried leaving my carriers out in our home with the doors open or removed, hoping my cats would see them as a safe place or hideaway. After the first few vet visits, Trinity, who is by far more intelligent than her brother, soon learned that she had been taken to the vet in that thing, and would not consider getting in it on her own. I now have to shut the doors to the bedrooms before I get the carriers out, so that I am actually able to get my cats in the carriers and to the vet by my appointment time. As I mentioned earlier I use a pheromone spray or *Bach's Rescue Remedy* before my cats are put in their carriers for travel. Check to be sure it will not interfere with any test or procedures for that appointment. Do not use on your cat without your vet's approval, especially if it is injured or it is an emergency visit. If your cat becomes completely over stressed about vet appointments, it is worth talking to your vet about giving a sedative before the appointment. Some cats can benefit from prescription medication to stay calm during stressful events like travel. Be sure

to tell your vet if your cat will be traveling on an airline, as altitude is thought to alter its response to some medicine.

The **vaccination protocols** have been changed in recent years, suggesting fewer vaccinations especially for indoor-only cats that are not in a multi-pet household. We may see recommended core vaccines for indoor-only cats continue to be reduced. Make sure you discuss your cat's lifestyle, age, and risk factors with your vet. Tell them the likelihood of your cat getting outside, and how many pets you have in your home, especially if those other pets are allowed outside. Tell your vet if you plan to show, board, or travel with your pet, as these are all factors to consider when vaccinating. You can check the American Veterinary Medical Association website at avma.org to get recent protocols, and see a diagram where they suggest your cat should be vaccinated.

Some vaccines are grouped together, making it hard to know what the initials and abbreviations stand for. The same vaccines are made by several different manufacturers. Vets, pet owners and breeders have seen different reactions in their pets. No company makes a 100% reaction free vaccine. Different manufacturers group different vaccines together, but most can still be ordered

RW SGC BoysnRags Maximus of PalaceCats
(blue point bicolor) at a show

Linda Dicmanis' Bingo (blue colorpoint)

separately as individual vaccines. Vaccines are grouped so that your cat can have fewer needle pokes, less risk of an injection site sarcoma (ISS), and because often certain vaccines are due at the same time. I had a vet special order a vaccine for my cats, because it was not one she normally purchased.

You vaccinate to give more immunity to disease, but vaccines do not prevent our pets from catching certain diseases; for example when humans get a flu vaccine and still get the flu. It is a good idea to write down the type of vaccine, the manufacturer, lot number and expiration date of the vaccine, the date given and the site or location on your cat's body where the vaccine was injected. The whole purpose of any vaccine is to make the body produce antibodies to certain diseases so that if it ever encounters the disease, these antibodies or memory cells are ready to defend the body against infection.

If you choose to vaccinate, you then have the question of whether you want booster shots, and if you do, how long between them. There are risks to giving no vaccines, the wrong vaccines, too many, too few or too frequently. If you give a booster vaccine too soon while the blood still contains antibodies to the original vaccination, the cat's body will actually

inactivate the booster shot, making its protection worthless. You can opt to have your cat's blood tested and **titers** checked to see if they still have antibodies present to some of the viruses. A titer measures the antibodies in the blood for a specific disease. Discuss titers with your vet before deciding the right choice for your cat.

In 2008 I changed vets when my two were given a combination vaccine in the scruff between their shoulder blades. Both of my cats had swelling and a reaction to the shots. I didn't know at the time, but it has been recommended that vaccines be given in a limb for years. The reason is simple— if a **vaccine associated sarcoma (VAS)** develops, the limb can be removed, likely saving the cat's life. When the vaccine is given in the scruff, the sarcoma or cancer is basically inoperable because it grows into the spine, chest and rib cage. These sarcomas are found in at least 1 in 10,000 cats. Some think the risk is much higher.

My current vet said that the sarcomas in the scruff are very hard to treat. He used octopus tentacles as an example, and said that it is hard to completely remove. The sad part is that a vaccine associated sarcoma in the scruff is completely avoidable, simply by giving the vaccine in the correct limb. I truly hope my cats do not develop a fatal

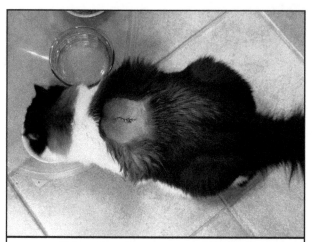

Tyler after the mass was removed
from between shoulder blades

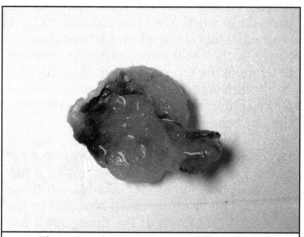

The mass that was removed from Tyler,
was about the size of a walnut

Tyler sporting his baby T-shirt after surgery

cancer because of the unwillingness of my last vet to follow the suggested guidelines. Both of my cats were very lethargic, did not want to be handled, and developed site reactions to their vaccinations.

Tyler's lump came back at the injection site. I had my current vet do a needle biopsy, and based on the results we decided to watch it. It grew slowly, but it did grow. When I scheduled their first dental I asked for the mass to be removed. Thankfully the pathology results came back as fatty scar tissue and not cancer but I am glad that it is out of his body.

There were a few complications after the surgery and it was a long few months of healing and baby T-shirt wearing to get him to leave the incision alone. I couldn't find just a plain T-shirt to fit him so I cut a few 12 to 18 month onesies and that seemed to do the trick. The pull-over worked better for us than the snap style. He weighs fifteen pounds and wore twelve month sizing. It was helpful to have several on hand so I could change them out often for one freshly laundered and sanitized. The E. collar would have kept him from licking but not scratching. After a month of putting Tyler in a T-shirt from his surgery, I tried two anti-lick products. You are not supposed to get those in the wound, which was hard not to do. He wouldn't leave the incision alone and slobbered drool everywhere after he licked the anti-lick products and his wound, I went back to putting him in the T-shirt. I started putting pure raw honey, a natural antibacterial, to promote healing on the area until the hair started to grow back and protect it from his rough tongue.

When your cat is going to be receiving vaccinations, it is a good idea to allow time to monitor them for any kind of reaction once you arrive home. I try to make appointments early enough in the day so that if a problem does arise; my vet's office will still be open. With Tyler and Trinity's past reactions to vaccinations, I choose to schedule separate visits, to avoid giving multiple vaccines at one time. I feel this is less stressful on their immune system. I am more cautious with them than I was with Skeamer, who never had an unwanted reaction to any of her vaccines.

There is debate about vaccines being live, modified live, killed, recombinant, adjuvant or non-adjuvant. Most breeders recommend killed or modified vaccines only. Some breeders void their health guarantee if certain kinds of vaccines are given.

The form of vaccination is determined by many factors, how the disease is spread, how prevalent it is, and how it is replicated in the body. The vaccine is not necessarily related to whether it is live, modified or killed. Some killed vaccines offer better immunity than some modified live vaccines do— it depends on the disease. It is something to talk to your vet about. The vet that I use now was very interested in the reaction Tyler and Trinity had to their vaccinations. I think that their reactions played a part in his recommendations of what to use in the future. I appreciate that he took my cats individual reactions in to consideration.

Live vaccines are the actual antibodies of the virus and are rarely used. The animal is given a live virus that has been made non-virulent, which simply means it is un-likely to cause the disease.

Modified live virus (MLV) vaccines means that the virus is alive and can replicate in the cat's body, but it has been modified as to not cause the disease, or at least not a severe form of it. Some diseases are simply too dangerous to allow to replicate.

Killed virus (KV) vaccines offer excellent protection. Some killed vaccines are also more likely to cause vaccine associated sarcomas or cancers, but most have now had the adjuvant removed.

Recombinant vaccines use a small fragment of the actual live virus or disease agent inserted into a harmless carrier virus.

Adjuvant vaccines are more likely to cause vaccine associated sarcomas and inflammation than **non-adjuvant** vaccines. The virus is added to other proteins and requires less of the actual virus. One problem with this is the animal's body can think it needs to attack the protein too. If the protein is like other cells in the animal's body, the body can actually end up attacking its own cells.

Check where you live to see if a **rabies** vaccine is required by law. I would probably choose to forego this vaccine on my indoor-only cats, but since it is a law and there is always the slight possibility of a rabid animal getting inside our home, they get it. I use the one year, non-adjuvant recombinant vector vaccine *Purevax* by Merial. It doesn't create as much inflammation as killed adjuvant vaccines typically do. I do know a Ragdoll cat that had a terrible reaction to a rabies vaccine and some breeders discourage it. There are documented cases of indoor-only cats contracting rabies. I have had problems in the past because our state requires the vaccine, and my vet at the time, would not keep my sick elderly cat overnight because her rabies vaccination was not current. A cat should always be healthy when given a vaccine, and it was not the right time to give her any vaccine, so she came home with me. Skeamer was aggressive, and this would pose a problem if she bit someone else. I was bitten for 17 years and knew she did not have rabies, but had she aggressively bitten another person without proof of a current rabies vaccination, my choices would have been limited. Rabies is a viral illness that attacks the nervous system and is almost always fatal. It is transmitted through a bite from an infected animal. My cats are indoors-only, but just to be safe my husband added a three foot high piece of clear *Plexiglas* over the screens on our slider doors, to keep another animal from coming in to any kind of contact with our cats.

Just as some breeders recommend certain vaccines, some recommend the type of anesthesia used during **surgery**. Anesthesia always comes with some risk. Be sure you remind your vet of any health issues your cat has before a surgery, all medications or supplements your cat is taking, and any reaction to medication or drugs it has had in the past. There are different kinds of anesthetic that can be used. Certain breeds are thought to be more sensitive to certain kinds. You should discuss the choices with your vet. They will use the best anesthetic protocol based on your cat's individual risk and what is appropriate for the needed procedure. Discuss the risk, and get instructions about what to watch for when you take your cat home. If you did not completely understand the dosing of medication, or you feel uneasy about how

it is to be given, it is better to ask again and verify the medication instructions than to give too little or too much. Simply being aware of possible side effects from surgery or anesthesia can give you more information to share with the vet in case something goes wrong. The more they know, the more likely they can accurately assess the situation. It would be a shame to just assume something was a normal reaction, when in fact, it was a sign of a problem that you did not know to watch for.

Before the surgery your vet will likely do an exam and ask if you want preanesthetic blood work done. I did not opt for this on my four and half month old kittens when they were altered, but I did when my ten year old cat was going to have a dental. The exam and blood work can help your vet determine if the surgery is safe to perform. Your vet may also order an electrocardiogram (ECG) prior to surgery, as cardiac abnormalities will not show up in a blood panel. There is thought to be an increased risk of

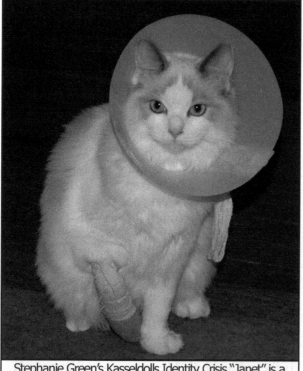

Stephanie Green's Kasseldolls Identity Crisis "Janet" is a blue bicolor, recovering after jumping onto a wood stove

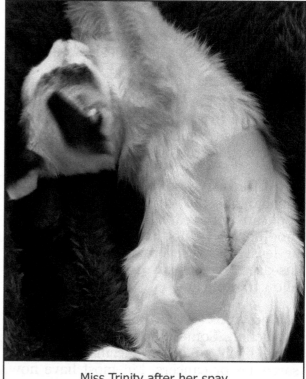

Miss Trinity after her spay

hypertrophic cardiomyopathy (HCM) in some breeds, including Ragdolls.

You can ask for an intravenous catheter to be used **during surgery** in case an emergency arises, your cat can quickly be given fluids or reversal drugs. The time saved in an emergency of already having the intravenous catheter in, may be life saving. This is especially important on long surgeries lasting over 30 minutes. Having the cat's airway protected with an endotracheal tube, eyes lubricated, and heat support all make for a more comfortable and safer surgery. With certain drugs used for anesthesia there are antagonist or reversal agents to bring them out of anesthesia quickly. Having a registered veterinary technician monitoring your cat's heart, oxygen, blood pressure, lungs, and temperature is also important.

When you take your cat home **post-surgery**, limit its area to run and try to keep it calm. I know that is easier said than done. I like to allow plenty of time to watch my cats after a surgery or vaccination. I will take a laptop or book, my cat's food, water and litter box, and we will camp out in the master bathroom or a small room, where I can easily watch them and keep them from hurting themselves. Anytime your cat has surgery you may be sent home with an Elizabethan Collar, or E. Collar (see photo far left). This cone-like collar is used to keep your cat from being able to pull at stitches or over-lick an incision.

It took Skeamer a long time to get over whatever they used to put her under, and I always feared that she could fall down the stairs, or fall trying to jump up on something. You should keep other pets and young children away from your pet during a recovery period. Your cat may eat less than normal but they should be drinking water and eating within 24 hours. Take note if your cat is unable to lie down comfortably, walk, eat, drink or use the litter box normally. Be sure to report redness, bleeding, puffiness,

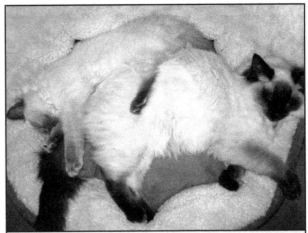
Linda Dicmanis' Bingo (blue colorpoint) and Schniffley (seal colorpoint)

Mary Becker's Tedrick "Teddy" (seal lynx mitted) and Toulouse "Touie" (blue point mitted with small blaze)

Mary Becker's Toulouse "Touie" (blue point mitted with small blaze) and Tedrick "Teddy" (seal lynx mitted)

Karen Wright of
Kylador's kitten

RockstarDolls
(blue cream bicolor)

Mary Becker's "Teddy"
(seal lynx mitted)

Karen Wilkinson's
Gizmo (cream bicolor)

Alissa Pendorf's Raina
(blue lynx bicolor)

PalaceCats MyGalSal
(blue bicolor)

Karen Wright of
Kylador's kitten

Karen Wright of
Kylador's kitten

pus or draining from the incision, trembling, seizures, lack of appetite, coughing, gagging, shallow, rapid or labored breathing or paralysis of the rear legs.

Our Skeamer, spooked as we were filling our aquarium, jumped from counter height, landed halfway across the room and ran upstairs. We continued cleaning the tank without giving it another thought. Later we handed her a bite of chicken, and she could not eat it. Skeamer always ate people food— yes I know it is frowned upon, but once you start it is hard to stop. I thought her inability to eat could be related to her cat acne, that we were told just to clean. I took her to the vet the next day and was shocked to find out she had broken her bottom jaw right in the center! My vet sedated her, and wired her bottom teeth together. The wire looped around her bottom teeth in sort of a figure-eight shape. She already had kidney problems at the time, and it took her quite a while to get over the anesthesia. Even in her

uncoordinated state, she had the wire off her teeth by that night, and I couldn't find the wire. I took her back to the vet and they did an x-ray to see if she swallowed it. Skeamer did not swallow it, but they chose not to redo the wire, and just let it heal by itself. This left me wondering why they did it in the first place, or didn't feel the need to rewire it the following day.

Upon telling this story to my veterinarian cousin, I learned the correct procedure actually involves running a wire through the bottom of the jaw and around the teeth in a figure-eight until the jaw heals. Also, with Skeamer already having kidney problems, she should have been given IV fluids to help rid her system of the anesthesia.

Believe it or not, I actually gave that vet another shot when Skeamer broke her tooth off biting me. I called them shortly after they closed, they told me to give her bread in case the tooth was lodged

Karen Wright of Kylador's kitten

Gail Vettel's of AngelKissed Ragdolls

Kylador's Murphey (seal point mitted)

RockstarDolls Ann and Andy (seal lynx and cp)

Karen Wright of Kylador's kitten

PalaceCats kitten (seal lynx mitted)

Karen Wright of Kylador's kitten

RocknRagz blue point kitten

in her throat, and to wait and call back after their phones went to the emergency number. Skeamer was in obvious pain. If she had swallowed the tooth I did not see the point of trying to make her eat bread. I hung up, decided to look for a new vet, and immediately took Skeamer to our closest emergency clinic.

Her tooth had broken off at the gum line, and they had to extract the remainder of the tooth and exposed root. No wonder she looked like she was in pain! They also suggested sending part of her gum off to pathology because it broke off. We got home six hours later. This is when we discovered trying to add canned food after years of only feeding kibble could be a problem.

Skeamer would not touch any wet food, yet we knew trying to crunch dry food had to painful. The best solution we could come up with was to water down her dry food. The pathology results all came back fine, but I think it is odd that Skeamer ended up with cancer on her jaw years later.

Skeamer started a funny little lip snarl (see photo bottom left) to keep her lip from going into her mouth after she lost that big front tooth. We soon discovered the snarl got bigger when she was not happy about something. I guess it was her "pitiful face" to get what she wanted— it worked most of the time.

RocknRagz' Mojo (blue bicolor)

Skeamer with her lip curled up "pitiful face"

Alissa Pendorf's Raina (blue lynx bicolor)

Feline Health, Illness and Disease

Gloie Wall's Benji (flame point mitted lynx)

Marsha Harris' Tess (seal mitted colorpoint)

I have had Tyler and Trinity at the vet's office more in the first few months after we brought them home, than I ever would have anticipated. In hindsight **pet insuranc**e of some kind or a program like *CareCredit* carecredit.com/vetmed services probably would have been beneficial. You can review and compare insurance online at petinsurancereview.com/cat.asp.

Dental disease can lead to many other problems, seen as early as age three. Dental checkups can catch problems early. If ulcers, decay, or infection are left untreated, the bacteria can affect the cat's whole body. The extra bacteria growth or related oral problems can damage the kidneys, liver, brain, heart, and joints. In addition to what you are doing at home for your cat's dental care, your veterinarian should do a yearly oral exam with intraoral radiography to check general health, and for oral problems, like feline stomatitis, or tooth resorption— both of which are painful.

The cause of feline stomatitis is not known, but it is suspected to be an allergic reaction to the bacteria in plaque. Plaque is the soft leftover residue on a tooth surface and tarter is the hard buildup along the gum line— both can lead to gum or periodontal disease. Feline stomatitis causes painful inflamed gums and may spread to the roof of the mouth and throat. Cleaning and steroids may help, but sometimes complete extraction of the teeth is needed. Tooth resorption, previously called feline oral resorptive lesions (FORLs) is the most common cause of tooth loss, and many cats with feline stomatitis also have tooth resorption. It is unfortunately a common problem in cats seven years or older.

In addition to visually looking at the teeth and gums for redness, red spots, tartar buildup, broken or brown teeth, inflamed gums, or bad breath, you can watch for behavioral changes. A cat experiencing dental problems may suddenly act aggressive or fearful of facial contact, exhibit excessive rubbing, shaking, pawing or scratching of its face, may yawn more than usual, turn its head to one side when eating, not want to or have trouble eating, stop grooming, have a poor coat, or drool excessively.

Tyler drools when he is happy or content, and has since he was a kitten. One of my cousin's cats did the same thing. If your cat

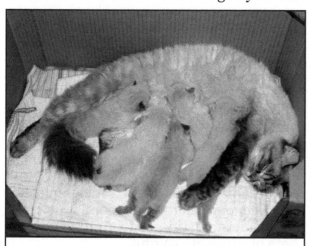

NenesRags Miley of PalaceCats (seal lynx point)

has always drooled when it is happy, there is probably no need to worry, especially if it has had an oral exam by your vet. Some cats just do this, but if your cat starts **drooling** and this is a new change, it is time for a vet appointment. Drooling can often be a sign that your cat has a problem with its mouth, is nauseous, or has an underlying health problem. You can read more about oral health at vohc.org.

A cat's normal **temperature** is 101.5 but between 100.5 and 102.5 is considered okay. It is easiest to take with a quick-read digital rectal thermometer. I use a disposable cover, and *K-Y* jelly to lubricate

the thermometer before I take my cat's temperature. I also find it best to wait until I have someone to help as sometimes two hands are not enough.

I watched my vet take my cats temperature. When I needed to take it at home, I called them and the vet tech refreshed my memory. I also found how-to videos online. Your vet can also show you how to do simple things like trim nails, check for dehydration, and give your cat a pill. I have learned you cannot put too much stock in the dry nose, wet nose, hot or cold ears theory to determine if your cat is sick. I have found my cats' noses are

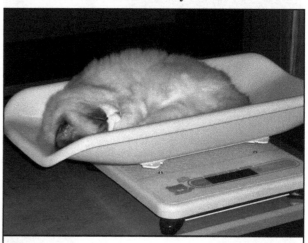

Karen Wright of Kylador's Watson

usually wet and I have felt their ears and feet temperatures change from hot to cold without them being sick. I heard in the Yahoo! cat group, that the ears and feet changing temperature are from them regulating their own body temperature. Skeamer used to leave sweat prints from her feet while at the veterinarians from being so stressed. I have noticed my cats want to be under the covers more in winter, and seek out the cool tile in summer.

A **scale** may not be on the "need" list, but it is nice to have. I was in the middle of replacing a broken one, and wished I had it for Skeamer. You can use a human scale and weigh holding your cat, then again by yourself and subtract to get the cat's **weight**. This is not as precise as using a baby, or postal scale. A pound or two drop in a human is not a big deal, but if a cat goes from 15 pounds to 12 pounds— that is a 20% drop in its weight. That would be equivalent to a person going from 120 pounds to 96 pounds. I weighed Tyler and Trinity most every week for the first two years of their lives. Trinity started out bigger than her brother, but in no time he outweighed her. Even after she leveled off, her brother's weight slowly kept climbing.

It is not uncommon for a Ragdoll to gain about a pound per month in its first year,

with its sides rounded out. This is harder to see with a long-haired cat. You should be able to feel the rib cage with moderate pressure. There is typically a significant difference in male and female weight, with males weighing more. Just like with the human population, the percentage of cats being overweight is growing. No pun intended. An overweight cat can have a shorter life span.

If you plan to put your cat on a **diet** consult your veterinarian first. After your cat's overall health is checked, you can do simple things to help it lose weight. Try to increase your cats fiber intake, add

Bridlepath Mercedes of Kylador
"Sadie" (seal bicolor)

Dollheaven Lexus of Kylador
"Lexie" (seal colorpoint)

then the increase will likely slow down. Ragdolls do not reach their full weight of 10 to 20 pounds until three or four years old.

Overweight cats can have more health problems, including diabetes, high blood pressure, heart disease, breathing problems, joint and ligament problems, arthritis, skin problems, urinary problems, or liver disease, plus increased problems with surgeries that require anesthesia. They also have a harder time doing everyday things like walking and grooming.

A good rule of thumb is to look down on your cat from above— it should not be convex

extra water to its food, increase proteins, decrease carbohydrates without adding more fat. If you feed dry kibble you can also try changing to a brand with a larger kibble size so eating takes longer. If your cat slows down to chew more it may realize it is full sooner. The best way to take weight off is with interactive play time. Make sure your cat always has water available when you are exercising it, and that you stop if your cat is panting, looks worn out or sits down.

You have more choices than ever before of where to buy your **cat medication**. The FDA has a list of things to look for when buying medication online, see fda.gov

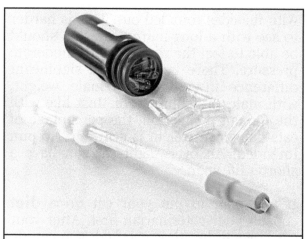

Bottle of empty gelatin capsules and
a piller with part of a pill in the end

and type in "online pet pharmacies." I unknowingly bought from one company that was not in the United States. If the product had arrived more timely I may not have looked so closely at the package and invoice. The product still had good dates on it, but buying outside the United States was one of the things to be aware of. A reputable company will require a prescription from your veterinarian for any prescription medication.

Giving a cat a pill or "pilling a cat" is not the easiest thing to do, and can leave both you, and your cat frustrated and stressed. You can purchase a piller (see photo above) that you place the pill in the soft end. It is like a syringe with a soft rubbery tip, that you use to insert the pill into the cat's mouth. I have better luck just using my finger. I had to pill my last cat daily, and my index finger became raw from the involuntary pokes from her teeth. She really was very good about it, but my finger skin just wore out. I got a rubber postal sorting tip, and cut the end off to slide it on to my finger, and it worked like a charm while still giving me the tactile feel of my own finger.

I found it the hardest to pill when my cats had to have metronidazole. Apparently it tastes terrible. Out of desperation, I

came up with the idea of putting it in clear gelatin capsules (see photo to left) to prevent it from being tasted. I put a dab of butter on the capsule and popped it right down their throat. Sealing the bad flavor in the capsule made it so much easier. You can find clear gelatin capsules at health food stores, specialty or compound pharmacies, or online. The smallest capsules I was able to find, size *#3*, were actually purchased from my vet. I have not tried the pill pockets yet, but may in the future. Many compound pharmacies can mix a prescription with a flavor, like fish, to help disguise its taste. This did not work with metronidazole, for me, with Tyler.

Sandy Baker's Rocky (seal lynx mitted)

I give my cats a treat after they get a pill, in hopes that following the pill with something they like will help it stay down. I have given a pill, knew it was swallowed, and found it on the floor shortly after. A pill that has been spit back up is usually so dissolved or slimy there is no way to give it again and you don't know how much medication the cat is actually getting. Some medications can be given in a topical solution which you rub in your cat's ear or apply with a transdermal patch.

With some pills I can crush them or open the capsule and sprinkle it on food, like L-lysine. Skeamer was on daily potassium for her kidneys. I could buy the potassium in powder form, but she would not eat it. I had to buy the potassium pills and crush them daily to get her to eat it sprinkled on her food. I usually gave her the potassium mixed with canned tuna, ham, turkey, or chicken. You do have to be careful when using people food to avoid giving too much sodium.

A cat will scratch itself to relieve an **itch** but not every itch is caused by fleas. It can also be an infection, auto immune disease, a mat in its fur pulling and pinching, a bad diet, allergies to food or even irritants to the same seasonal things we are allergic to.

Sandy Baker's Pippin (seal mitted with blaze)

Your cat may get temporary relief from itching by soaking a washcloth in black or green tea, letting it cool then holding it on the hot spots for a few minutes. In my opinion, finding the cause and treating it is better than just treating the symptoms with anti-inflammatory drugs like steroids. If you are bathing your cat you may want to switch to perfume and dye-free or oatmeal shampoo.

Cats can have **allergies** to the same things we do, including ingredients in food. Allergy testing is hard to do on cats. Most people try using a process of elimination. I do not know if Trinity

is actually allergic to grains, but her breathing, eye and nose discharge are all much better on grain-free foods. Look for your cat scratching, licking or biting at its feet, avoiding its food, mouth ulcers, or becoming sick after eating food containing certain ingredients. You may see an improvement in the condition by feeding a limited ingredient diet, adding omega oils, probiotic, regular grooming, antibacterial medications, steroids, immunotherapy, stress reduction methods for behavioral issues, or acupuncture.

Omega oils come in different qualities or grades. The company should use pure pharmaceutical grade oils that have been filtered to assure that you are not feeding your cat high levels of chemicals or toxins such as polychlorinated biphenyls (PCB), heavy metals or mercury. It should be certified to meet safety standards. If the omega oil DHA/EPA is derived from fish, the smaller the fish usually equals the smaller the amount of mercury. Cats have a limited ability to convert alpha-linolenic acid (ALA) essential fatty acid, which is derived from plant sources to eicosapentaenoic acid (EPA) and docosahexaenoic acid (DHA).

Cats can get **feline acne** from allergies although it is more commonly associated

Kylador Canadian Chloe (blue bicolor)

with eating from plastic dishes. Cat acne is basically clogged pores and it is largely preventable by not using plastic feeding bowls, by good hygiene and grooming. It can also be caused by overactive oil glands, bacteria, allergies and even stress. In the early stages it looks like blackheads but can progress to infected itchy red bumps often on the chin, face or lips. It is more common during the spring and fall. You can keep the area clean by brushing fine food particles out with a flea comb. Once acne is present, typically cleaning with diluted peroxide, vinegar, *Epsom Salt*, or a prescription antibiotic soap is recommended. If left untreated, it can get serious enough to need veterinarian treatment and antibiotics.

I guess this is a good time to go over **human allergies** to cats. I have heard it said that Ragdolls shed less than other cats, or that they are hypoallergenic. Their hair is not what causes the allergen, it is the Fel d 1 protein, found in the cat's saliva that creates the dander when they groom themselves, and Ragdolls have this too. The dander is what most people are allergic to.

Some breeds are thought to produce less of the problem protein, like the Siberian, which produces little to no Fel d 1. Even the Sphynx is not **hypoallergenic**. They just don't have the same amount of hair for the dander to stick to, so the dander wipes off their skin easier than cats with lots of hair. The Balinese, Oriental Shorthair, Javanese, Cornish Rex, Devon Rex, LaPerm, Russian Blue and Sphynx are thought to produce less of the Fel d 1 protein. Un-neutered male cats produce more Fel d 1 than neutered males and both produce more than females. It is thought that light colored cats produce less than dark colored cats. I know that I can see more dander on Tyler, but I am not sure if he produces more being seal colored and male, or if I just do not see it as well on Trinity's mostly white coat. Maybe someday with science and

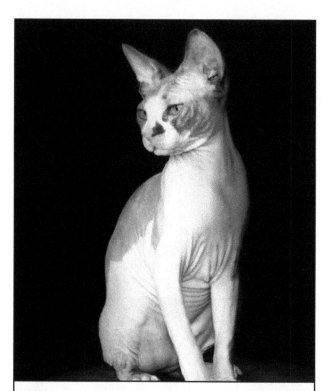
This Sphynx is Blue Berry Smoothie of PalaceCats

specific breeding we could have a breed that produces none of this protein; giving allergy sufferers a chance to own a cat without the allergy symptoms.

The same vacuuming, bathing, and washing that you do for parasite control is also your most effective way to rid your home of cat dander. There are bath wipes that can help without giving your cat full regular bath, like the ones by *Allerpet*.

There are studies that show having a pet as a child will actually reduce the likelihood that you will become allergic as an adult. I guess it is just like being exposed to a small amount of an allergen over time makes your body have less of a reaction to it. I know this is true with my husband and his poison ivy outbreaks each year. Some people's allergies are so bad they choose to take shots and still own cats. I thankfully do not have many allergies that an OTC antihistamine can't handle, but my husband's allergies are much worse than

Marsha Harris' Quincy (flame bicolor)

recently added a cat ancestry test to identify 29 breeds, including Ragdolls.

There is no way to reverse the damage to a gene that has experienced mutation. The animal will pass the mutant gene to at least some of its offspring. Mutations can be dominant or recessive. A dominant mutation will result in the disorder. If the animal receives the recessive gene, it may appear unaffected but it is still a carrier. Learning these gene characteristics, and not breeding carriers, is wonderful information for preservation of breed health. Ragdolls are not prone to many health issues, but if I was buying from a breeder I would want to know that my cat and its parents were not carriers for hypertrophic cardiomyopathy (HCM) or polycystic kidney disease (PKD).

Your cat should not have frequent diarrhea or vomiting left untreated, as both can lead to **dehydration**. To check for dehydration using the skin turgor test, grasp some skin in the scruff at the base of your cat's neck. If it stays up without springing back, your cat is dehydrated. The more severe the dehydration the longer it will take the skin to return to normal. Knowing how to look for symmetrical pupil size, healthy gum color or return of color after pressing on the gums, and taking your cat's temperature, are some things a pet owner can and should learn to do correctly. Ask your vet before an emergency; they are a knowledgeable source and will more than likely be glad to show you these simple things you can do at home. Not to micromanage, or replace your vet by any means, but to provide you the ability to give extra information to your vet when a problem does arise.

mine. In spring and fall when his allergies are at the worst, I try to clean the house more often, and wipe our cats down more. It probably would have been wise to make our bedroom feline free, but I just could not shut the door on those pitiful feline faces, or sleep through the pawing at our door.

DNA testing or deoxyribonucleic acid testing is relatively inexpensive and can provide a wealth of information. It can tell you inherited traits, disease risk factors, gene related disorders, genetic information, such as color, and even parentage evaluation. You can order a test yourself online from catgenes.org or vgl.ucdavis.edu. You send them a swab from your cat's cheek, the cat's hair or have your vet do a blood draw following the detailed online instructions, and you get the results mailed back to you.

For dogs there has been a test available to identify some breeds. UC Davis has

*Y*ou know how your Ragdoll acts, better than anyone else.

Sometimes you may not know what is wrong, but you know that something is not right. There is a website, vet.cornell.edu/fhc with helpful information and how-to videos for basic care.

A **hairball** or trichobezoar is regurgitated hair from the digestive system. All the ones I have seen looked like a tightly compressed wad of hair usually surrounded in a puddle of liquid that came up at the same time. Even though my three cats have been different colors, the hairball is often dark colored and actually resembles feces lying in liquid until I get closer to clean it, and can tell it is tightly packed hair. The hair is consumed while grooming and most of it is passed in the litter box. If your cat is vomiting often or for an extended period of time a trip to your vet is needed.

Cats should not have frequent **vomiting**, a hairball now and then, yes; vomiting— no. Often simple diet changes are enough to upset a cat's stomach, but it can be a sign of a more serious problem. Information about any recent changes should be relayed to your vet. If the vet can find no reason for the repeated vomiting, I would search the house for signs of anything your cat may have ingested, or a chemical it may have absorbed through its paw pads. See the list of household dangers in the chapter "Dangers and Emergencies." I would also make sure your cat had plenty of fresh water, and switch its food to a limited ingredient food, to rule out food intolerance. Not only can your cat become allergic or intolerant to a food it has been eating; the cat food industry is not exempt from food contamination. If you suspect your cat is simply trying to vomit up a hairball, you can give a product like *Laxatone* or hairball remedy treats, but vomiting should not be a common occurrence.

Repeated vomiting left undiagnosed can have deadly consequences. Often vomiting is a sign of a stomach or intestinal disorder

Sandra Baker's Rocky (seal lynx mitted)

Nancie East's Reilly (blue cream / blue tortie)

or a systemic illness. Your vet will likely collect blood and urine samples to rule out a disease or an illness like kidney or thyroid problems. In younger cats it is more likely that something that should not have been ingested was indeed swallowed. String, thread, or a toy part, can cause serious damage or a blockage to your cat's intestines. X-rays, anti-vomiting drugs, and IV fluids may be a part of a vet visit, and sometimes even an ultrasound or endoscope may be needed to find the cause. As a last resort exploratory surgery may be needed.

With **diarrhea** or **constipation**, the first step is a visit to the vet. Self-treatment and home remedies can delay proper treatment. Diarrhea could be a symptom of a parasite, viral or bacterial infection, inflammation of the bowel possibly from food allergies, organ failure (liver, cardiac, or kidney), a neoplasm (mass, tumor or cancer), or metabolic (diabetes or thyroid).

Marsha Harris' Quincy (flame bicolor)

Cats can also have **inflammatory bowel disease**, **IBD**. If left untreated the vomiting and diarrhea can cause dehydration, weight loss and even death. With IBD, the walls of the intestines or stomach get inflamed. Diet changes, probiotic, antibiotics and anti-inflammatory drugs can help with the symptoms, but there is no cure for IBD. **Irritable bowel syndrome**, **IBS** is not a disease but a physical problem usually brought on by stress or anxiety causing similar symptoms to IBD, like diarrhea.

Antibiotics destroy bacteria and can upset the flora, or good bacteria balance. A **probiotic**, which restores good bacteria, should not be given within two hours of an antibiotic. Some warn against overuse of probiotics causing diarrhea and some tout its uses to helping with skin issues, cat acne, inflammation and fatigue.

It took several episodes of Tyler having diarrhea and vet visits with cultures,

Marsha Harris' Tessie (seal point mitted)

Alissa Pendorf's Raina (blue lynx bicolor)

If frequent **diarrhea** is a problem for your cat, take it to the vet, along with a recent stool sample. It is a good idea to rule out gastrointestinal worm parasites with bowel problems. If the stool sample test comes back negative it does not mean your cat is parasite or worm-free, because there are times, at different stages, that it may not show in a sample. Not all dewormers treat every worm or parasite.

Both of my cats were dewormed twice. I was told that cats have egg larva in their bodies, and that high stress can actually make the eggs hatch, so I was taking a fecal sample to the vet every time Tyler had diarrhea, before I realized that he just had sensitive bowels. Tyler's results always came back with clostridium, which cats have in their system anyway. There is speculation that a cat having parasites early in life may cause the gut later in life to become sensitized to protein.

before I realized he just has a sensitive nervous stomach when he gets scared, like when we have company. I start giving him the probiotic, *Fortiflora* before company arrives and plain unspiced canned pumpkin or squash. You are supposed to be able to feed plain yogurt, cottage cheese, or boiled chicken and rice to help with diarrhea also, but my boy would not eat any of those. Check with your vet about giving slippery elm, acidophilus or other probiotics.

Plain pumpkin, squash, papaya and cat grass are good sources of fiber. I wish that pumpkin came in smaller cans, because I seem to throw out more than my cats eat. I have tried to freeze it but when thawed the consistency seems different, and my cats do not like it as much as a newly opened can at room temperature. I have tried feeding them organic baby food squash, with nothing added. It comes in a more usable size than the cans of pumpkin and is another good source of fiber. They loved it... the first time.

Tyler gets diarrhea from some antibiotics, including amoxicillin. They actually make the situation worse, so metronidazole, the generic for *Flagyl*, became the drug of choice for him. My vet also said I could give *Pepto-Bismol* or *Kaopectate*, but both contain bismuth subsalicylate, a salicylate which contains aspirin, and should not be given in large amounts. Plain *K-P* (kaolin and pectin) is available from some pet places. My vet also prescribes *Carafate* for Tyler's diarrhea, which is actually an ulcer medication. I did not see any bad side effects from it, so I give it in addition to the metronidazole. A few breeders in the Yahoo! groups say *IAMS Hairball Formula* food, and *Benebac* probiotic are also very helpful.

If your cat has not been on antibiotics recently ask your vet to run a feline diarrhea panel comprehensive test. This **polymerase chain reaction** (**PCR**) test is sometimes called a DNA test. This comprehensive diarrhea panel can detect salmonella, giardia, campylobacter, cryptosporidium parvum, clostridium perfringens enterotoxin, tritrichomonas foetus (TF), toxoplasma gondi, feline coronavirus (FeCoV), and feline panleukopenia virus (FPV). Tritrichomonas can be overlooked or mistaken for giardia, both are protazoan parasites. *Ronidazole* is used to treat tritrichomonas, but it is not actually approved for use yet in cats, and you may have to give your consent for your cat to be treated with it. *Ronidazole* should not be handled by women without wearing gloves. Remember that changing the kind of cat food or left over soap residue from washing food or water dishes can cause diarrhea also. Toxoplasma gondi is the parasite that could be harmful to the fetus if you are pregnant. See more about this in the chapter "Litter and Litter Boxes."

A lot of the same things that help with hairballs, or diarrhea will help with constipation because of the fiber, but too much fiber can make it worse. Some people give petroleum, or oils like vegetable, olive, or cod liver oil. High levels of petroleum has been linked to other health issues. There are medications to help with frequent constipation, but exercise, plenty of water, foods high in protein, and less filler should also be helpful. Some suggest having cat grasses like oat grass available. Be sure to check with your vet beforehand.

Feeding at specific meal times will get the cat's digestive system to contract more than it will free-feeding. Keeping your cat's weight in check will also help with bowel issues, but keep in mind that other medical issues or medications can also lead to constipation.

Chronic constipation can lead to **megacolon** which causes the colon to stretch and lose its ability to pass feces. Megacolon occurs more in males and in cats older than six although it can develop on its own. Signs of megacolon are a decrease in appetite, weight loss, vomiting, lethargy, and a hard or sensitive abdomen. Often, diet change to either a high fiber or easily digestible diet is recommended along with laxatives, stool softeners or drugs

Sonja Phillips' Tucker Bee (seal point mitted)

that help your cat pass the feces. Your vet may have to give enemas or even perform surgery to remove feces depending on how compacted the cat is, and the amount the other methods worked.

For 21 years I have been a cat owner and happily did not know firsthand about my cats' **anal glands**. Tyler changed that. At least one of my cats starting peeing over the edge of the litter box, I assumed it was Tyler since he's the larger cat. I changed to taller, larger litter boxes. This brought another unwanted change— pooping outside the box. I thought it could be because of the new boxes, so I cut larger openings in the new litter boxes. Over the next few weeks I noticed less fecal output and Tyler started licking his genital area. Then once again, there was poop outside of the boxes. Knowing that changes in litter box usage often occur because of a medical problem, I took Tyler to the vet. He was the one licking and has more sensitive bowels than Trinity. The vet felt his abdomen and looked at his genitals, took his temperature and said he was fine. Tyler continued the same behavior. One evening the licking became more frequent, so I checked for anything unusual, and two small bubbles of foul smelling, grayish paste was coming from his anal sacs. I researched on the internet and learned that cats usually do not have problems with their anal sacs because they are typically emptied as the cat defecates. Tyler had been going to the bathroom less, so his sacs filled up. With this new information, I returned to my vet, and Tyler's anal sacs were expressed. I didn't want to change their food and they had stopped eating the pumpkin and squash some time ago, so I asked my vet if I could just add fiber, like *Metamucil* to his food and he confirmed that was okay.

I'll go back to the saying that you know your cat better than anyone else. When you see licking or a change in litter box use, there is often an underlying cause. Hopefully the added fiber will increase Tyler's bowel movements, and if so, his anal glands should stay emptied on their own.

Ideally you should never need to concern yourself with your cat's anal glands, although overweight and under-active cats may have more problems. They serve no real purpose other than marking your cats stool with its scent. They can be removed if your cat has repetitive blockages or is unable to empty them. Blocked or impacted glands can lead to impaction, abscess and infection. Watch for obsessive licking or scooting.

External Parasites, Parasitic Worms, Fungus, and Bacteria

There really is a disease called cat scratch fever or **cat scratch disease**, CSD. It is a bacterial infection transferred from an infected cat to humans with a bite or scratch. Kittens are more likely to carry the bacteria than adult cats, but your cat can get the bacteria from flea and tick bites, or blood transfusions. Symptoms in cats include severe anemia as the red blood cells break down and can even cause death. In humans the symptoms can last from two to four months and may include a mild infection at the site of the bite or scratch, swollen lymph nodes (especially those around the head, neck, and arms), possible fever, headache, fatigue and poor appetite.

The disease is more of a problem in individuals and felines with a compromised immune system. With CSD, it is believed that infected flea feces gets into open wounds. You can reduce your risk by avoiding rough play with your cat, washing

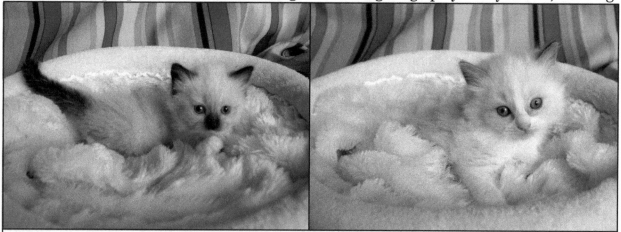

PalaceCats Moonlight Dancer (seal mitted) female, and PalaceCats Max E Moo (blue bicolor) male

to disinfect bites or scratches immediately, and not allowing a cat to lick any open wounds you may have. It is also possible to transfer other bacterial infections like MRSA, therefore treat all cat scratches with caution, and watch for signs of infection. For all cat bites, seek medical attention.

External parasites, like fleas, ticks, mosquitoes and mites, can all pose health risks to your cat and your family. On the flip side, so can pyrethroid, citrus d-limonene or permethrin containing **spot-on treatments**, especially on kittens or elderly cats. Take precaution with products containing organophosphate insecticides (OP's) and carbamates containing ingredients such as: carbaryl and propoxur chlorpyrifos, dichlorvos, phosmet, naled, tetrachlorvinphos, diazinon and malathion. Consider using insect growth regulators (IGR's) that are not pesticides or insecticides. Using products containing adulticides and IGR's that kill fleas in all life stages is the key to keeping a flea problem at bay.

*N*ever use a spot-on flea treatment made for dogs, on your cat.

Fleas can multiply quickly, and they feed on blood. When a flea bites, it leaves protein from their saliva. Many cats are allergic to the protein. Not only will it make them itch and scratch, which can cause bleeding, inflammation and infections— it can also cause permanent hair loss. A large number of flea bites can make a cat anemic. Anemic cats often eat dirt or litter, trying to ingest more iron.

There are a few insecticides, imidacloprid, fipronil, and selamectin that have fewer toxic side effects on the nervous system. They can be found in *Advantage, Frontline, Top Spot* and *Revolution*. Some spot-on treatments protect against fleas, flea eggs, ticks, mosquitoes and prevent heartworm. Most websites that sell these have a comparison chart to make choosing easier. Some places will not sell the spot-on medication that prevents heartworm without a prescription from your vet.

Bathing your cat immediately before or after using a spot-on treatment is not recommended. Be careful with flea shampoo even if it is labeled "natural" because they can still cause allergic reactions. Remember to rinse well with any shampoo. There are also preventatives that you feed your pets. I would definitely talk with my vet first, as some of these contain garlic.

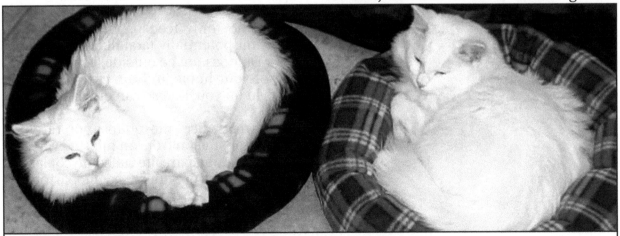
Patricia Besaw's Bellapalazzo Sir Bentley and Bellapalazzo Maximillion (both BEW, blue-eyed white)

Sandy Baker's Pippin (seal mitted with blaze)

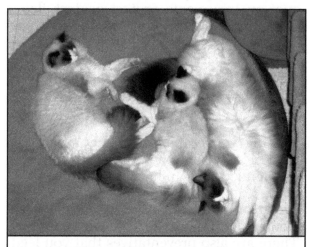
Karen Wright of Kylador's three bicolor Ragdolls

Bridlepath Mercedes of Kylador "Sadie"
(seal bicolor) with nursing kitten

Too much garlic can cause red blood cell damage and anemia. Grooming, bathing, vacuuming, and washing are much safer. I have also heard that *Borax* or food-grade diatomaceous earth (DE), sprinkled on the carpet works on flea control. Do not buy the pool filter grade DE, which is heat and chemically treated. DE can be a problem if inhaled or large amounts are ingested.

I will not use a flea collar on my cats, but if you have a flea problem, it can't hurt to add one to the canister or in the bag of your vacuum, to kill the fleas collected. When I wash my cats' bedding, I use the hot sanitary cycle, with bleach and double rinse. I find the bedding with removable washable covers easier to wash than laundering the whole bed. There are also washer balls that act like *Velcro* in collecting cat hair. I use them in every load except for my delicates. I do not see any harm in using them and even if they remove some of the hair, it is that much that is not going into my septic system or dryer vent. The only downside is you have to pull the cat hair off them.

Fleas can pass along parasites and diseases. For example, when a flea eats tapeworm eggs from an infected cat's stool, and then moves on to another cat, the flea is ingested by the cat during grooming; the swallowed eggs can develop in to a tapeworm.

Ticks not only feed on blood, they can transmit potentially fatal illnesses. Even if your cat does not go outside, you go in and out of your home and can carry fleas and ticks in on you, and so can other pets.

Ticks, fleas, lice, mosquitoes, or rarely a blood transfusion from an infected cat, can also transmit a parasite called mycoplasma haemofelis or previously haemobartonella felis. The parasite or mycoplasma organisms, closely related to rickettsia, infects the red blood cells causing the cats own immune system to destroy the red blood cells in an attempt to remove them. The red blood cells are what carry oxygen in the body. This is called feline hemotropic mycoplasmosis or feline infectious anemia (FIA). It is more severe in cats with feline leukemia (FeLV), or feline immunodeficiency virus (FIV). Stress can reactivate the infection, and like most infections, it is found more often in sick, young, or elderly cats. Signs are anemia, depression, lethargy, weight loss, pale gums and sometimes even jaundice.

Without treatment, a third of the cats with a severe infection will die. Some of the cats that recover become carriers. A carrier is not really contagious if the blood sucking parasite problem transmitting the organism is controlled. It was harder to diagnose before PCR testing because the amount of infected cells showing up on a blood smear can vary greatly from one time to the next. Treatment is three weeks of tetracycline or similar antibiotic to kill the mycoplasma, and a steroid to suppress the immune system to slow down red blood cell depletion.

When you groom your pet, feel for ticks, and use a flea comb to check for fleas and little dark specs of flea dirt (flea feces) they leave behind. If you are not sure if it is just dirt, or flea dirt, you can put it on a white paper towel and wet it to see if it turns red, which flea feces will do. If you see evidence of fleas, or even one flea, you can bet there are more you are not seeing.

To remove a tick, get tweezers and grasp the tick close to where its head goes into your cat's skin and not by the tick's body. Do not twist or squeeze. Put the tick in a jar of rubbing alcohol to kill it and then disinfect the bite wound with soap and water or an alcohol wipe. You want to remove ticks as soon as you find one because the longer it stays attached, the more chance your cat could have diseases transferred to it. Be sure you get the whole tick, head and all. If the head breaks off from the tick's body

and remains in your cat, you need to take your cat to the vet.

Grooming time is a good time to check the ears for **ear mites** and overall health. Ear mites are a parasite. They are not as common in adult cats or indoor-only cats, but left untreated they can cause yeast or bacterial infections, and with extreme cases can actually rupture the ear drum. Look for ear scratching, head shaking, or a smell from the ears. If ear mites are present, you will likely see dark waxy deposits like coffee grounds inside the ears. Your vet will probably clean the ears to remove the majority of mites, and then prescribe medicated drops for you to apply at home. Ear mites require medicated treatment that must be administered for the prescribed time to rid the ear of mites, and to prevent a secondary bacterial or yeast infection. Even if it looks better, you should have your vet take a sample of material from the ear and check under a microscope to be sure the mites and their eggs are gone. With indoor-only cats there are other likely causes for ear scratching; like allergies, excessive wax production, bacterial or fungal infections, parasites, foreign object in the ear, sunburn, skin cancer, or polyps. If you notice a change with your cat's ears it is best to let your vet determine the problem and treatment.

It is possible to get **ringworm**, also known as dermatophytosis, from your cat, or vise-versa but it is not actually a worm. It is transferred by contact from an infected source, and cats can carry ringworm on their fur. A small percentage of ringworm infections will illuminate under a black light, but a fungal culture is usually required to diagnose an infection. Cats are more likely than dogs to show no signs of infection, like raised circular lesions or hair loss. Ringworm is more often seen on kittens or cats with a weakened immune system and children more so than healthy adults.

If this fungal infection is transferred to humans, it produces red circular raised lesions on the body. It was once thought to be a worm because of the shape seen on the skin. It cannot be prevented, but you can treat it with an antifungal cream on humans, and dip or shampoo for cats. You have to be diligent because it is not the easiest fungus to get rid of. It requires thorough cleaning of the contaminated areas, in addition to treating your cat and humans infected.

There is a three course feline vaccine that can be given after your kitten is four months old that protects against the most common forms of the fungus however it is not recommended as a routine vaccine due to questionable efficiency.

For your health and your cat's health, keeping external parasites at bay and deworming for internal parasites is part of the care you need to provide. As kittens, most will get a dewormer. Your

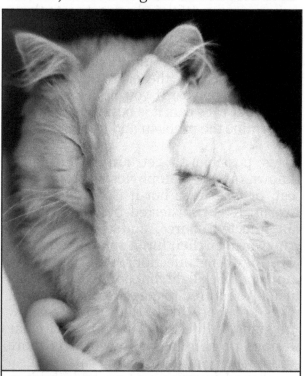

Karen Wilkinson's Fred (cream bicolor)

vet can also test for **internal parasites** like roundworms, tapeworms, hookworms, lungworms, and heartworms. Keeping your cat inside only, well groomed, off the kitchen counters, as well as keeping litter boxes well cleaned and using basic sanitary cleaning methods will go along way in prevention of these unwanted parasites.

Most parasite infections come from ingesting other animals, like mice or birds infected with parasites, infected larva in the environment, animal feces, or from external parasites. Cats allowed outside are much more likely to be infected. To clear an infection, the egg to worm cycle has to be broken. There is a prescription topical dewormer you can give at home in a stress free environment, based on weight.

Symptoms of **intestinal worms** are a pot belly appearance, diarrhea or vomiting (sometimes with blood), weight loss, dull dry coat, anemia, weakness, and of course, actually seeing the worms. If left untreated, some worms can cause convulsions, pneumonia, intestinal obstructions, and blindness, although blindness is very rare. Most veterinarians suggest bringing a stool sample to your appointment for it to be checked. It takes different medication to get rid of various types of worms.

Roundworms (ascarid) are found in the digestive tract absorb nutrients and interfere with digestion while damaging the lining of the intestines. They can be several inches in length, and resemble spaghetti that you can sometimes see in vomit or stool, (sorry for the visual that I just created). In people the symptoms may be mild or very obvious. People infected may be irritable, fatigued or restless, have a loss of appetite, anemia, weight loss, diarrhea or abdominal pain, swollen lymph nodes, difficulty breathing, a cough, or blurred vision.

Tapeworms (dipylidium caninum) also absorb nutrients from the cat's intestines.

Segments of the worms can sometimes be seen near the cat's anal area. If the segments are dry, they look similar to grains of white rice. In people the symptoms are similar.

Hookworms (*A.* tubaeforme) attach themselves to the wall of the cat's intestines and feed on the cat's blood which can cause life-threatening anemia. In people hookworms often show up on the feet as an itchy rash but they may also cause a cough, anemia, or intestinal problems.

Feline **Lungworms** (aelurostrongylus abstrusus) are contracted through ingesting the larva, often by eating snails, slugs or another animal that has eaten the infected snail or slug itself. After migrating to the lungs clinical signs are respiratory system related, but are rare. However, when the eggs laid in the lungs, hatch and the larva crawl up the trachea, coughing is very common. This leads to them being swallowed for later defecation into the environment.

Heartworm (dirofilaria immitis) in cats can cause lethargy, asthma, vomiting and death. Cats can get heartworm in any area or location that dogs can get heartworm including those kept indoors. Heartworm is transmitted by mosquitoes. Infected mosquitoes are in almost every state, with the southern states being hit hardest. Infected animals were moved to new homes after hurricanes *Katrina* and *Rita*. The relocated, infected animals allowed mosquitoes to transmit heartworm in more areas.

I did not think we had many mosquitoes in our home, and assumed we didn't need to protect against heartworm or fleas. Our cats are indoor-only, without another animal in the house going in and out. We usually use the air conditioning and seldom open our windows, and even when we do open them, they all have screens. After I started using a preventative on my cats,

I made a mental note when I saw, heard, or killed a mosquito, and there were more than I thought that made it inside.

My veterinarian cousin, Dr. Shaylene Snyder, informed me of documented cases that made me rethink my cats' safety from heartworm. Where I live, in North Carolina, a study showed that almost 55% of cats diagnosed with heartworm were indoor-only cats. That was startling and scary to me. She did say I should have my cats antigen and antibody tests done, and then start using *Revolution* monthly preventative. Ms. Trinity showed more possible symptoms, and asthma was suspected, but both tests came back negative.

The tests are not perfect, and some infections are not detected. The antigen test only detects adult female worms, and the antibody test is not foolproof because it takes weeks for the antibodies to show up— then eight months after infection, the cat can test negative for antibodies.

Gloie Wall's Jamie the Sheltie with Katie

Kylador As You Like It "Basil" (blue bicolor)

Patricia Besaw's Bellapalazzo Maximillion
(BEW, blue-eyed white)

Dogs have a treatment for heartworm, but sadly that same treatment can be potentially fatal for cats. The outcome of managing the symptoms with steroids and antibiotics, surgery to remove the adult worm, or non-treatment can all be very risky. Some cats clear the infection on their own, naturally with their immune system, but with no present cure, the percentages are pretty low of a cat surviving heartworm. Even if the disease is treated, your cat may experience severe complications, or even death, when the worms die. In cats, even juvenile worms can damage the lungs.

Some cats have a life-threatening immune reaction called **HARD**, **heartworm associated respiratory disease**. Adult heartworms can be up to six inches long, causing inflammation and releasing toxins when they die. An infected cat can die suddenly of respiratory failure when a blood clot blocks off blood supply to the lungs.

The best action is to keep your cat inside, use a protection treatment monthly, and not get heartworms in the first place. The preventatives do not keep your cat from being bitten, but they do kill the heartworm when they are in the first larva stage. Heartworms in cats do not need to develop into adults to cause serious heart damage.

Feline heartworm is often overlooked or misdiagnosed as asthma or allergic bronchitis, as the symptoms can mimic those and other diseases, such as pneumonia and digestive problems. It is possible that an infected cat will show no symptoms. Chronic signs you may see over a longer period of time include vomiting food or foam (not related to eating), gagging, anorexia, lethargy, weight loss, coughing, difficulty breathing, panting, open mouth, or rapid breathing. Acute or sudden onset symptoms are diarrhea, vomiting, fainting, wobbling, convulsions, seizures, difficulty breathing, collapse, blindness, or rapid heart rate. Sudden death may happen before an accurate diagnosis is made.

Infections and Diseases

Asthma also called allergic bronchitis or bronchial disease can be life threatening if left untreated. Rapid breathing or your cat coughing, that may be mistaken for your cat trying to vomit a hairball, and only producing foamy mucus, are a few of the signs to look for. If you suspect asthma, your vet can test and come up with a treatment plan for managing it. Home care may include oxygen, metered dose inhaler (MDI), nebulizer treatments, administering steroids, or use of bronchodilators. Things you can do to help in addition to medicating:

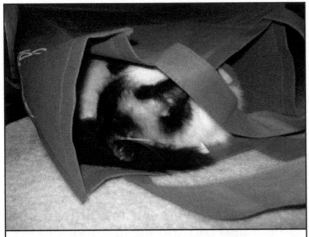

Linda Dicmanis Schniffley (seal colorpoint)

VancyDolls Hello Dolly "Dolly" of GuysnDolls
(seal mitted)

change to a less dusty litter, change food, change cleaners used, clean your home of dust, pollen and mold, use a HEPA air filter, and not submitting your cat to secondhand smoke. A good website for learning more is felineasthma.org.

Feline **upper respiratory infections**, **URI** diseases like viral rhinotracheitis, feline herpes, calicivirus, and pneumonitis, also called chlamydia psittaci or more recently chlamydophila are airborne viruses and are highly contagious. Chlamydophila infections are less common than viral respiratory infections.

URI's primarily affects the eyes, causing conjunctivitis, or swelling and discharge in one eye, then the other. It can cause sneezing, and a runny nose, but not the full range of signs associated with feline viral rhinotracheitis, FVR, also called feline influenza or the cat flu. While we are speaking about the flu, I should mention that it is highly unlikely, but not impossible, to transfer a virus like the flu between humans and cats. Cats are more likely to get the bird flu or H5N1, from eating raw bird meat.

There are several different strains of both feline viral rhinotracheitis, FVR and feline calicivirus viruses, FCV. They have symptoms like a common cold or

flu. URI's can be treated with antibiotics, but left untreated URI's can be fatal. Infected animals are highly contagious to other cats, and may show either severe or chronic respiratory signs. These diseases spread through direct contact, through the air by coughing or sneezing, or human contact if the person has been close to an infected cat.

Feline herpes virus, **type 1**, **FHV-1**, is the most common viral infection. It is also known as the cat flu or FVR, an upper respiratory infection. It is estimated that up to 80% to 90% of cats in the world are infected with feline herpes virus FHV-1. Some may be only be carriers and not show symptoms.

Feline viral rhinotracheitis, **FVR**, an acute respiratory disease is typically only fatal to young or elderly cats. With older cats, the main risk lies in obstructed nasal passages blocking the smell of food, causing loss of appetite. It can also develop into a bacterial infection.

FHV-1 is difficult to distinguish from **feline calicivirus viruses**, **FCV** without a PCR test. Dual infections are common but FHV-1 often has corneal ulcers while FCV typically causes oral ulcers. FCV usually affects the throat, eyes, nasal and oral cavities, and sometimes the lungs or intestines. It can be complicated by anorexia and dehydration. There is a virulent strain of FCV that can cause ulcers on the paws, lameness and even arthritis. Antibiotics do not work on viruses but are useful for secondary bacterial infections.

The symptoms between the two are very similar. Both are easily spread from body secretions or discharge from the eyes, nose, and mouth. Sneezing and coughing can send infected droplets up to four feet. It can also be spread by contaminated dishes, litter boxes, or even your own hands. The virus can live for up to 48 hours on objects. Places with high cat populations, such as catteries, shelters and multi-cat households, are more susceptible to an outbreak. Once a cat has herpes, it has the virus for the rest of its life.

Vaccination against FHV-1 can prevent development of severe diseases, but it does not always protect against infections. Early symptoms usually include conjunctivitis (eye infection), sneezing, and discharge from the nose and eyes. The symptoms can develop to include fever, lethargy, loss of appetite, a spastic cough and severe eye infections complicated by painful corneal ulcerations that may result in blindness. As long as an infected cat receives adequate food and water, the fairly mild condition will run its course in seven to ten days. The infection can be reactivated when your cat is stressed. Eliminating stress, using a humidifier or saline nasal spray occasionally during a flare-up, and making sure your cat is eating and drinking, will all speed the recovery. If your cat's symptoms do not seem to be clearing up, or if there is blood in the discharge, you may need to get antibiotics to fight off a secondary bacterial infection, eye ointment for ulcerative keratitis, or decongestants to decrease nasal discharge. If a flare-up becomes severe and is left untreated the tear ducts may scar over and cause damage to nasal passages.

There are antiviral drugs available, which may be something to discuss with your vet.

Trinity is suspected of having feline herpes but at times I wonder if it is simply a food allergy because her eyes and nose always look much improved when she eats grain-free food. Since it is not curable I have not had her tested, but there are tests available. I use humidifiers in winter. I attempt to use saline in her nose but she really hates that so most the time I just clean her eye corners and nose with a sterile Q-tip. I also add 500 mg of L-lysine to her food daily for several weeks at a time. There is a new treat that contains L-lysine, but

Ms. Trinity's eye

my cats do not seem to mind it sprinkled on their food. If she seems uninterested in her food, I heat it in the microwave to make the smell stronger or add some of her much loved *Whole Life,* or *Halo Liv-a-Little* dried or water soaked chicken treats on top.

Without L-arginine, an amino acid found in most foods, herpes cannot reproduce. L-lysine, also an amino acid suppresses the herpes virus ability to replicate. High amounts of L-lysine will decrease the herpes virus use of arginine. Arginine is essential to the processing of protein. Cats with arginine insufficiency cannot convert ammonia to urea, and can have an excess amount of ammonia in the blood, which can lead to renal failure. Vaccinating a cat that already has herpes is a possibility. Typically, you do not vaccinate a cat that is not healthy, but in the case of herpes using the ocular (nasal) vaccine, you can produce extra immune stimulation to the nasal area where the herpes infection is active which may help reduce the signs of infection. This was never offered for Trinity.

Feline infectious peritonitis virus, **FIP/FIPV**, is unfortunately poorly understood, although there have been lots of recent developments in understanding the virus. There is only one licensed

Laurie Nicholson of RocknRagz' Rory
(flame point mitted)

FIP vaccine available; however, this controversial modified live vaccine has minimal, if any effectiveness in preventing FIP, and it is not generally recommended by the American Association of Feline Practitioners Feline Vaccine Advisory Panel. The risks and benefits of vaccination should be weighed carefully. Cat owners should consult their veterinarian to help them decide if their cat should be vaccinated.

The common and benign form of feline coronavirus is referred to as **feline enteric coronavirus**, **FECV/FeCoV**. FECV is in a cat's intestines where it causes little harm until it mutates and attacks the cats

own immune system. Any cat infected with the harmless FECV has the potential of it mutating in to FIP. They do not know why the virus mutates in some cats, and not others. The majority of cats with FECV remain healthy, although they may shed the virus in their feces. Only a small percentage of cats that are exposed to the feline coronavirus develop FIP. This can occur weeks, months, or even years after initial exposure. Most cats do not "catch" FIP, but develop it themselves from their own mutant FECV, although FECV spreads readily from cat to cat. The virus can persist in dried feces or on cat litter for three to seven weeks. Thorough cleaning of litter pans and spilled cat litter with common household soaps, detergents, and disinfectants, neutralizes the FIP virus.

The FIP virus can take two forms, wet or dry. The wet form involves an accumulation of high protein yellow fluid in the chest or abdomen. The dry form, which does not have fluid, is characterized by inflammatory lesions called pyogranulomas that can be found in almost any organ of the body, including the nervous system. The dry form of FIP is harder to diagnose but in mild form, the drug polyprenyl immunostimulant (PI) by Sass & Sass used to treat feline herpes is showing promise. FIP symptoms can mimic symptoms that are similar to those of many other diseases. FIP may cause difficulty breathing, lethargy, vomiting, diarrhea, and loss of appetite, a low-grade or fluctuating fever that is not responsive to antibiotics, chronic weight loss, depression, anemia, and is almost always fatal.

A cat that has been vaccinated for FIP or any of the coronaviruses, will test positive. That is one reason FIP is usually diagnosed on clinical signs. At Auburn University in Alabama, clinical pathologists can now do a sensitive fluid test that is more sensitive than others, although it is still not a definitive diagnosis. There is no simple diagnostic test, no way to screen healthy cats for the risk of developing FIP, nor a foolproof way to diagnose FIP in sick cats. Since diagnosing FIP should never be based on any single test result, veterinarians will gather a variety of information to help them rule out other diagnoses. Typically FIP is not actually confirmed, it is diagnosed by exclusion of other diseases. Biopsy, blood work, ultrasound and x-rays, may all be used, but many cases are not confirmed until a postmortem necropsy is performed.

The most susceptible are young kittens, cats six months to two years old, elderly cats with a less vigorous immune system and cats in cat-dense environments like shelters, multi-cat households or catteries where large numbers of kittens and adult cats share living space. In multiple cat environments, keeping cats healthy and minimizing exposure to infectious agents decreases the likelihood of cats developing FIP. Litter boxes should be kept clean and located away from food and water dishes. The litter box should be cleaned of waste daily, and the box should be thoroughly cleaned and disinfected regularly. Newly acquired cats, and any cats that are suspected of being infected should be kept separated from other cats. Preventing overcrowding, keeping cats current on vaccinations, and providing proper nutrition, and sanitation can help decrease the occurrence of FIP. FIP cannot be spread from your cat to your dog, as it is specific to cats.

If you lose a cat to FIP, you need to thoroughly clean your home with diluted 1% bleach to water solution and discard bedding, litter boxes, and pet bowls that the sick cat used. Not all items can be cleaned with a bleach solution, so to be on the safe side, you should avoid getting another cat right away. The virus can live on for months on items that you are unable to disinfect.

Laurie Nicholson of RocknRagz' Abby Rose (blue bicolor) and Bindi Lou (seal tortie mitted)

Mary Becker's "Touie" (blue point mitted with small blaze) and "Teddy" (seal lynx mitted)

Nancie East's O'Malley (chocolate lynx mitted) and Murphey (flame colorpoint)

Feline panleukopenia, **FPV**, commonly known as feline distemper is a highly contagious viral disease. The virus is very stable, and is resistant to many chemicals. It may remain infectious for as long as a year at room temperature. Cats of any age can be stricken, but like most diseases, the young, sick, elderly or not adequately immunized, are the most susceptible. After exposure to the virus, many of the cat's white blood cells are destroyed, making it susceptible to bacterial infections and other complications.

There are vaccines for this virus that are an effective preventative but must be administered before your cat is exposed. The panleukopenia virus is similar to the parvo virus in dogs. The virus can be transmitted through infected fecal waste, but may be present in other body secretions. It is spread by contact with humans, infected cats, clothing, food bowls, crates, or cat carriers. Typically outbreaks happen during the warmer months, and where groups of cats are together, like kennels, pet shops, and shelters. Because this virus is widespread, most kittens are exposed to it within their first year.

The signs can vary from mild to extreme, and often come on suddenly. An infected cat may have diarrhea, loss of appetite, vomiting, depression, lethargy, anemia, hang over their water dish, dehydration, seizures, weight loss, and a sudden high fever of 104 to 107 degrees Fahrenheit, followed by a low body temperature shortly before death. Often once the sickness is discovered it can go on for days, or in advanced cases, it may cause death within hours. Some pet owners think their cat has been poisoned or has swallowed something poisonous.

Feline immunodeficiency virus, **FIV**, is similar to human acquired immune deficiency syndrome like AIDS, but it is not the same virus and cannot be passed from cats to humans. This virus attacks the immune system. Signs can include chronic infections that do not respond to treatment, respiratory problems, loss of appetite, persistent diarrhea, and severe oral infections. FIV is passed from cat to cat, primarily through bites. A vaccine is available to help protect cats from contracting FIV, but this vaccine is not recommended if your cat is indoors-only without an infected cat in the household.

A FIV blood test should always be performed before vaccination. A PCR blood test is available to determine if your cat has been exposed to this family of viruses and can differentiate between a vaccinated cat and an infected cat. Keeping your cat indoors will reduce the chances of it fighting with another cat that may have FIV. The FIV test is not always conclusive before the kitten is nine weeks old, and it may need to be retested. Kittens younger than six months can show a false positive from antibodies from the mother cat. This is especially true with kittens from unknown origin, or a shelter, as an FIV positive mother cat can pass it to her kittens. Kittens from a breeder where the mother is FIV free, are not as likely to contract the disease.

FIV cats can live for several years. The biggest threat is actually a secondary infection or kidney failure. Treating these other problems promptly is even more important with a FIV positive cat. If the cat is not showing signs of FIV, it is still important to make sure your cat is eating a healthy high protein diet. You may want to speak to your vet about adding vitamins, antioxidants, omega-3 and omega-6 fatty acids. You should make sure that any new kitten or cat added to your home is FIV free if you have other cats at home. The virus is generally spread from biting, saliva to blood. It is possible, although not as likely, that the virus can be spread from cat to cat by grooming, or eating and drinking from the same bowls.

Feline leukemia virus, **FeLV** is a fatal infectious virus usually causing death within a few years and more often kills young kittens than adult cats. It affects the immune system and can increase susceptibility to other diseases, secondary infections and several forms of cancer, in addition to leukemia. It is transmitted through the urine, saliva, and feces of infected cats. There are blood tests to determine if your cat may be carrying the virus. Like FIV your cat should be tested before being vaccinated against the disease and the test is not conclusive in kittens younger than six months old. Since there is no cure, it is best to keep your cat indoors and away from contact with other cats that may be infected. There is no link between feline leukemia and human forms of leukemia. Signs of feline leukemia include recurring or chronic illness, weight loss, unusual breathing patterns, lethargy, diarrhea, fever, and a yellow color in the whites of the eyes and around the mouth.

The USDA has approved a drug for treatment of FIV and FeLV. It is not a cure, and will not work on all cats. It is called Lymphocyte T-cell Immunomodulator (LTCI). It is manufactured by T-Cyte Therapeutics, Inc and is distributed by ProLabs and IMULAN BioTherpeutics. LTCI helps lessen the symptoms by stimulating the cats own immune system to fight the virus, improving the quality of life in infected cats.

Feline lower urinary tract disease, **FLUTD**, usually occurs in cats between two and six years old. It happens in both male and female cats, but male cats have a narrower urethra, and tend to be more prone to obstructions than females. These obstructions can be very serious and can even be fatal. The causes of FLUTD can be inflammation, diet, stone formations, obesity, viral or bacterial infections, stress, and anatomical abnormalities.

The symptoms are frequent trips to the litter box, prolonged squatting or straining to urinate with little output, failure to use the litter box, urinating in unusual places, especially smooth surfaces, blood in urine, dehydration, lack of appetite, excessive licking the genital area, crying while urinating, vomiting or depression. If you notice a strong ammonia-like, or unusual smell to your cat's urine there may be a problem.

When other issues have been ruled out, a cat with urine issues may be diagnosed with FIC or feline idiopathic cystitis. It is a inflammatory condition that seems to be stress related.

Signs are similar to urinary tract infections, stones or blockages. Often pain medication is prescribed along with looking for ways to reduce your cats stress, and adding more wet food and water.

FLUTD can develop into more dangerous problems like **stones** or blockages. It was thought that ash in a cat's diet was associated with FLUTD, but ash does not cause FLUTD. The amount of magnesium proportion of ash seems to be more important. A diet low in ash could be deficient in calcium and still high in magnesium. Today's cat food is formulated to minimize the formation of struvite stones, a matrix of ammonium-magnesium-phosphate. There downside to this is an increase of calcium oxalate stones.

If your cat is prone to stones, a canned or wet diet will probably be recommended. Diets and feeding schedule can also affect the urine acidity or alkalinity. A high pH level (alkaline) of 6.8 or above tends to allow struvite crystals to form. The pet food industry responded by acidifying or lowering the pH of cat foods to prevent the development of struvite crystals. Acidifying urine pH results in more calcium loss into the urine— these factors lead to calcium oxalate stone development. Recently calcium oxalate stones have been on the rise, and they cannot be dissolved with special diet like struvite stones. Surgery is usually needed to remove stones that are too large to pass, especially in male cats.

Calcium oxalate stones are typically seen in cats between five and fourteen years old. These cats may show an acidic urine pH, hypercalcemia (elevated blood calcium), but may not have crystals in their urine or bladder infections. Struvite stones are almost always related to bladder infections in cats.

After a cat eats, it tends to have an alkaline tide. The urine's pH is increased three to five hours after a cat eats, and then after several hours it returns to the acidic range. When a cat is free-fed the peaks and valleys in pH are minimized. Most food manufacturers are aiming for a neutral pH to try to prevent both types of stones, but genetics is also being researched as a cause. FLUTD can have several contributing factors, so diet alone cannot claim to prevent it, but the amount of water intake does seem to play a role. Switching to filtered water is best if stones are a problem and you may find an increase of water intake using a plug-in water fountain system. Diet change alone is not a cure-all, and is not appropriate for all urinary problems. Your vet should recommend appropriate action to prevent future

stones, including treatment with possible antibiotics, anti-inflammatory drugs, diet, supplements, holistic or homeopathic remedies. Foods that say "designed for urinary tract health" or advertise having cranberries added, are not necessarily the same as food that is correctly pH balanced.

Feline **diabetes** can be a very serious disease with no cure. In most cases it is, manageable with diet change or diet change with medication, depending on whether your cat is insulin dependant. There are two types of diabetes, type 1 and type 2, with type 2, being seen most frequently in cats. Type 1 is insulin dependant and requires insulin in addition to diet change. Type 2 is non-insulin-dependant and can usually be managed with dietary changes to high fiber, low carbohydrate canned food. In some cases your cat may even go in to remission from the disease.

Males, elderly and overweight cats are the most affected. Keeping your cat a normal weight is important as many cats become diabetic due to obesity. Diabetes changes the way the cat's body regulates blood sugar or glucose. A normally functioning pancreas will produce insulin that allows glucose in the blood stream to enter the cells, and get used up as energy. The pancreas of a diabetic cat does not

Sandy Baker's Rocky (seal lynx mitted) drinking water from a *Drinkwell*

produce enough insulin. After the glucose builds up in the blood, it is excreted in the urine. Excessive blood sugar can cause blindness, chronic infections, kidney and liver deterioration, neurological problems, and sometimes causes weakness in the back legs, coma, and death.

Symptoms to watch for are weakness, depression, rapid weight loss, increased thirst, urination, or appetite. The symptoms may not be noticeable until the disease has progressed; therefore routine blood work and veterinarian visits can help diagnose diabetes early, avoiding more serious complications.

Pancreatitis is an inflammation of the pancreas, a glandular organ that is under the stomach and the first part of the small intestines. The pancreas has two functions; exocrine— to produce the enzymes needed to digest food, and endocrine— to produce hormones, including the hormone insulin, which help the uptake and storage of glucose (sugar) and amino acids (proteins). The inflammation causes a leak of the digestive enzymes and then the pancreas begins to literally digest itself.

Pancreatitis can happen suddenly or over time. Pancreatitis is serious and can be life-threatening, especially if it is the acute or sudden form. Cats more often have the chronic form which develops over time, making it harder to diagnose. The exact cause is not known but high fat meals, obesity, contaminated water or food (salmonella or campylobacter), some drugs or toxins, other diseases, medications or infections are thought to be risk factors.

Symptoms are loss of appetite, weight loss, dehydration, vomiting, painful abdomen, fever or below normal temperatures, diarrhea or depression. Your vet will likely ask about your cats eating history, perform a physical exam, along with blood test or a radiograph to out rule a

blockage. Treatment includes resting the pancreas, IV fluids, pain management, and diet change.

Liver disease or liver failure is usually fairly advanced before any signs are noticed. Liver disease is often found in conjunction with other diseases like pancreatitis, hyperthyroidism, diabetes, congestive heart failure, FIP, IBD, cancer or very rarely, Cushing's syndrome. Since the function of the liver is similar to other organs, the symptoms can be like other diseases and may require more than one test to diagnose. Liver disease can be caused by other diseases, bacterial infections, worms, parasites, stress, abrupt change or surgery, and rarely, persistent gallstones.

Liver failure is very serious and requires immediate veterinary attention. Life without a functioning liver is not possible; although it is possible, for the damaged part of a liver to be removed,

BoysnRags Sir Oliver of PalaceCats (blue bicolor)

and the liver to regenerate itself. A cat's liver converts waste in to a substance the kidneys can remove from the body. It regulates chemicals, amino acids, sugars, fats and proteins in the blood, produces bile to aid in digestion and proteins for blood plasma.

A cat with liver failure will likely have jaundice. You may see a yellowing of the eyes, ears or gums. Other symptoms are abdominal swelling, a reduced appetite, refusal to eat, increased water intake, increased urination, vomiting, diarrhea, weight loss, lethargy, seizures, irritability or depression. A high protein diet which balances minerals and vitamins is usually prescribed to lighten the work of the liver. Often a feeding tube is used for up to eight weeks. There are also drugs that can be used and fluids given to help flush the system of built-up toxins. The treatment greatly depends on the cause of the liver failure and the extent of the damage to the liver.

BoysnRags Sir Oliver of PalaceCats (blue bicolor)

High blood pressure or **hypertension** is often seen with other health issues like kidney, diabetes or thyroid problems. If hypertension is left undiagnosed or untreated, it can lead to a detached retina, blindness, damage to the brain, kidneys, heart, or blood vessels.

I recently read that if a detached retina is treated very quickly it may be possible for some of the vision to be restored. I regret not stressing more to the vet about how Skeamer's eyes were getting worse. She started being afraid of shadows on the floor, and we noticed if we were hand feeding her, she no longer went right to the food. The vet we had at the time thought it was just cataracts or old age eyes. She ended up going completely blind around age fifteen. I will say that the ol' girl was able to learn "whoa," "go right," and "go left" which I found pretty impressive. We also made sure we did not move anything around in the house or leave anything on the floor. We made steps to the sofa and bed so she didn't have to literally jump blindly.

None of my vets ever checked Skeamer's blood pressure. The two times I asked for it to be done, it did not happen. The first vet I asked did not have blood pressure equipment and the second vet had equipment, but could not do it. High blood pressure was suspected because of her kidney failure, her loss of sight, and the new occasional howling during the night. When my current cats are around age seven, or if they develop thyroid, kidney, or eye problems— I will ask for their blood pressure to be checked with a Doppler unit.

Thyroid problems are suffered by humans and felines alike. Testing for thyroid problems is done with blood work and should be part of any senior cat's blood panel test starting at age seven because early in the course of this disease the cat may be without symptoms. If caught early and treated early the better the outcome.

Hyperthyroidism is an overactive thyroid that often leads to the cat being underweight. It is common in cats over seven years of age. Symptoms to look for with hyperthyroidism are an increased appetite or activity, fast heartbeat, nervousness, irritability, changes in behavior, weight loss, vomiting, diarrhea, increase in water consumption, frequent urination, hair loss, neglected coat, tremors, weakness, labored or rapid breathing, and howling at night. These symptoms can mimic several other medical issues. Hyperthyroidism can also contribute to heart disease, high blood pressure or liver disease, and is thought to have a detrimental effect on joints and ligaments.

Hypothyroidism is exceedingly rare, and is seen much less often in cats than hyperthyroidism. Hypothyroidism is an underactive thyroid usually resulting in the cat being overweight. Hypothyroidism can cause liver and heart problems. Symptoms include weight gain, lack of appetite, slow heart rate, excessive thirst, excessive grooming, hair loss, a dry and dull coat, dander, constipation, behavioral problems, lack of energy, or lethargy, cold intolerance, mental dullness and sometimes aggression or failure to use the litter box. Treatment choices are daily medication, surgery to remove the damaged thyroid or radioactive iodine treatment.

Hypertrophic cardiomyopathy, HCM, is the most common feline cardiac disease and can lead to congestive heart failure, blood clots and death. It can be an inherited or an acquired disease but is often secondary to hyperthyroidism. HCM is an abnormal heart muscle function. Typically the left ventricle is the most affected, but as it gets thicker it causes the atrium to work harder and become larger, which causes the valve between the two to leak. When the heart's pumping ability is diminished, the walls of the heart become weak, enlarged, or thickened.

Karen Wilkinson's Myst (blue colorpoint) and Gizmo (cream bicolor)

Some of the signs to watch for are the inability to exercise, fatigue, fainting, poor appetite, or trouble breathing, and weakness or limb paralysis, seen more often in the back legs. Blood clots can develop and get lodged in the legs, called saddle thrombosis. This is a life threatening condition with a very poor prognosis and must be treated quickly. The excess fluid may collect in the lungs, abdomen or limbs, and clots may develop along with congestive heart failure.

In a cat with heart problems, if fluid has started to buildup in their lungs, they may be reluctant to lie down or may sit more upright in an attempt to make themselves comfortable. Some cats do not show signs if the cardiomyopathy develops rapidly. Most cats with HCM will develop a heart murmur. Often times if a kitten has a heart murmur, it will outgrow it by six months of age, but in Ragdolls and Maine Coons a DNA test is a wise idea.

Thickening of the heart muscle or hypertrophy can be caused by other diseases also, like high blood pressure, congestive heart failure or hyperthyroidism. There is no cure for HCM but there are medications and supplements to slow the advance. There is a blood test, *Cardiopet* proBNP that can measure the peptide released by the heart when it is stretched. You can have your cat DNA tested for HCM. If your cat tests positive for the genetic mutation, you should follow up with an echocardiogram.

A negative test does not mean your cat cannot still develop HCM— it just means it is negative for the mutation.

A positive result for the mutation does not mean your cat will definitely develop HCM.

HCM can be found in all cats, domestic and wild, purebred or stray, however it is found more in middle-aged cats and in male cats, and is more common in the Maine Coon and the Ragdoll. In 2005 researches at UC Davis found a mutation in the DNA of Maine Coons called A31P. Recently they found the R820W mutation in Ragdolls; both are mutations of MyBPC3 myosin binding protein *C*, which is an important cardiac muscle protein. Cats with the MyBPC3 mutation are believed to be more likely to develop HCM; and cats with the mutation affecting both copies of the gene tend to have a more severe form of HCM.

Genes come in pairs. If one gene is affected, it is heterozygous for the mutation. If both genes in the pair are affected, it is homozygous for the mutation. The research is promising for understanding the genetic causes, in hopes of treating HCM cats with gene therapy. In humans it is believed that there are multiple gene mutations that can cause HCM, and I think they expect to find more than the two MYBPC mutations in cats also. I would want to know my cats sire and dam had been tested within the last one or two years, and still tested negative for this mutation, or any other disease.

Polycystic kidney disease, **PKD**, is another genetic disease that a DNA test can test for. An ultrasound can also be preformed to see if there are cysts in the kidneys. It is in the Ragdoll line because of breeding that has been done with Persians and Himalayans. PKD is a progressive disease of the kidneys. It is characterized by the presence of multiple cysts in each kidney. The cysts grow and enlarge in the kidneys, reducing their ability to function correctly. PKD itself shows no symptoms until it has progressed, causing renal failure. Renal failure caused by PKD does not show different symptoms than renal failure not caused by PKD. There is not a cure at this time, but it is largely preventable by not breeding PKD positive cats. Although rare, kidney cyst can be attributed to factors other than heredity, such as trauma or infection.

Signs are weight loss, vomiting, depression, excessive urination and thirst, lethargy, and enlarged kidneys. Some things like diet and supplements used for kidney failure may help slow down the growth of the cysts and help with kidney function. It is possible for cats to only have one kidney— this can be determined with an ultrasound.

Chronic renal (kidney) failure, **CRF**, is a leading cause of death in older cats. It is also called chronic renal insufficiency (CRI). Kidneys eliminate waste from a cat's body. When the kidneys begin to fail, they are no longer able to filter waste properly, which basically poisons a cat with its own waste. The nephrons in the kidneys die off and can no longer rid the body of waste and keep the electrolytes processed, which results in an imbalance. The kidneys job is to filter waste, specifically urea and creatinine from the body, regulate salts or electrolytes like potassium, calcium and sodium, make erythropoietin that produces red blood cells and stimulates bone marrow, and produce rennin, which controls blood pressure and urine output. The failure and deterioration of the kidneys can also cause other problems like high blood pressure or anemia.

Subcutaneous, or **sub-Q fluids** are typically recommended because they help flush waste from the body. ACE inhibitors, calcium channel blockers, and anti-depressants, used as appetite stimulators like mirtazapine, are also looking promising, as does, *Azodyl* and L-arginine. The sub-Q fluids can be given alone or have medication added. Some of the medication increases blood flow to the kidneys or corrects an electrolyte imbalance, and some lower blood pressure. A person in the Yahoo! Ragdoll group told me her vet recommended using *Amphojel*. This aluminum hydroxide antacid was not recommended to me by my vet, but it is supposed to be given with food and help bind phosphates, reducing the phosphorus intake. In some cases a kidney transplant is an option. This is one disease that receives extensive research— new tests and studies seem to be ongoing.

CRF is thought to be more prevalent in some breeds— thankfully the Ragdoll is not one of them. The cat's age, genetics, diet, dental disease, blood pressure, hyperthyroidism, HCM, PKD, diabetes or other diseases may all contribute to CRF. This is one reason I had on my list of questions earlier in the book, about knowing if your cats sire and dam had both kidneys.

From about age seven on, your cat should have its blood tested as part of its annual veterinary exam, or sooner if you notice any CRF symptoms. Symptoms to watch for are an increased thirst and urine output, licking lips, halitosis (bad breath), nausea or gagging, grinding or cracking sound

of the jaw, vomiting, drooling, hunched over their water bowl, dehydration, constipation, loss of appetite, weight loss, muscle deterioration, poor hair coat, lethargy, weakness, depression, sound sensitivity, oral ulcers, detached retina, or eating litter. At the end stage of CRF you may see convulsions, low temperature, coma and then death.

Most cats are not diagnosed until after symptoms are noticed, and by then a significant amount of their kidney function has likely been compromised. Diagnosis is made by blood work, urinalysis, abdominal ultrasound and sometimes radiographs.

My Skeamer (DLH, domestic longhair)

Unfortunately, I know a little about feline renal failure, but thankfully Skeamer's levels were caught early in a blood test, and progressed slowly. I feel that knowing it was a problem from a blood test when she was around ten years old, before she showed any signs, gave us a huge advantage in making changes to help her.

Generally a low phosphorus, low sodium, low protein diet, high in omega fatty acids, with soluble fiber, and increased antioxidants is recommended.

We changed her food to *Hills Prescription Diet Feline KD*. Skeamer would not eat canned food which would have been better for her with the extra water content. I have heard that you cannot really increase a cat's consumption of water and that if you add moist food, it will drink less water than it will on dry food. In hindsight, I wish I would have purchased a water fountain to encourage her to drink more water, and I wish I had started her life feeding wet food instead of just dry. Over time we added potassium, omega oils, and a blood pressure medication for suspected hypertension.

When she was diagnosed, I felt like I was going to lose her right away. It was near Christmas and I was beside myself with worry. The vet stressed that it was caught early and to simply change her food. I did not hear about giving sub-Q fluids until many years later, and even then, the vet thought the food change, supplements and meds were enough. Maybe they were. Our Skeamer was not a Ragdoll and she didn't enjoy being held or cuddled. Sitting through a Sub-Q treatment for her would have been hard, simply being still and contained. Toward the very end of her life, I learned about *Azodyl* but Skeamer already had other health issues and was 16, and I felt like we were stuffing enough pills in her as it was.

I was told that renal failure often exists with high blood pressure and thyroid issues, and that the three often go hand-in-hand. I bought books on what to expect and things to watch for in an elderly cat with renal failure. There are several simple things you can do, like raising the food and water bowls to help prevent oral ulcers and adding extra litter boxes. She would flood the litter box, sometimes with very strong smelling urine. Her thirst never seemed to increase, she did not vomit often, and her fecal output was dry, but it always had been. Her coat didn't look straggly until after she was elderly.

ARF, or **acute renal failure** is extremely serious, but if caught right away, sometimes normal kidney function can be restored. ARF is typically caused by a urinary obstruction, infectious disease, trauma or ingestion of toxins. The most commonly ingested toxin is antifreeze or lilies. ARF can quickly become fatal. Immediate veterinary treatment is immensely important.

There are more than 200 types of feline **cancer** identified. Cancer is a leading cause of death in felines. Cats are far more likely to develop cancer than humans, even though cancer is prevalent in people. Early detection is still the best protection. Cancer is an abnormal growth of cells and can happen anywhere on, or in the body.

While grooming or petting your cat, take time to feel for any lumps or masses. A large percentage of masses or tumors found are cancerous. Early spaying or neutering and keeping your cat out of the sun, will help lower your cats risk of certain cancers. Some cancers, like abdominal cancer, are harder to detect early and you will have to watch for signs such as vomiting, lethargy, loss of stamina, decrease in exercise, diarrhea, weight loss, bleeding or discharge, offensive odor, lameness or stiffness, urinary or bowel changes, abnormal swellings or growths, sores that do not heal, rough hair coat, increased water intake, difficulty in moving, urinating, defecating, breathing, eating or swallowing. You probably noticed that these signs, are the same as many other diseases, and does not necessarily mean that your cat has cancer.

As cats age, so do the chances that they will get cancer. Most of the time, the cause is not known, other than with vaccine associated sarcomas (VAS), or injection site sarcoma (ISS). The cellular make-up, or type of cancer, is needed to determine the treatment and prognosis.

A cancer diagnosis was once considered to be a death sentence. Now there are treatment options depending on the type of cancer, where it is, if it has metastasized (spread), and the overall health and age of your cat. Treatment is typically surgery, chemotherapy, radiation therapy, or a combination. You can also seek out a veterinary oncologist for specialized cancer care.

Let me jump in here with another personal story. Skeamer had been living over six years with kidney failure that had progressed slowly. In January, when she was almost 17 years old, I found a lump on her chin the size of a pencil eraser. She was blind by then and I watched the lump for a week just to make sure she hadn't missed her step and bumped her chin on the coffee table. The hard lump did not go away. I took her to the vet and she said it looked like cancer, but due to Skeamer's kidney levels, she did not recommend any form of treatment. She also did not give me any time frame or any idea of what to expect in its progression. I wish I would have asked for a biopsy, or at least asked what to expect, the time frame and likely progression of this apparently cancerous lump. I left that day thinking it must be no big deal, and that her kidneys would likely fail before the cancer was a problem. The lump grew very quickly and by April, just after her birthday, she suddenly had pain when eating.

Her grooming habits had deteriorated over the last year and she seemed to re-adjust herself while napping more, as if she wasn't comfortable. She had long hair, and it was hard to tell, but we thought she had lost weight. At the time we were going through medical problems within our human family, and I guess I was just naive as to it being related to the lump on her chin. The night she could no longer eat without pain, I knew it was time to end her suffering. I had false hopes that it was just a bad tooth, but when we got to

the vet's office the next morning, the vet agreed that it was time to let her go. After she was euthanized the vet looked more at her jaw. The cancer had actually spread and broken the jaw bone and was taking over part of her tongue.

In hindsight, I wish I had asked more questions. Depending on the kind of cancer and the rate it grew, I may have opted to have it removed due to how slow her kidney levels had progressed. I simply had no idea that the cancer could spread that fast, break bones and cause painful eating in four months time. Even if I had been given all the facts and chosen not to do any radical cancer treatment, I could have started giving her pain medication, to keep her more comfortable and stopped giving her kidney medication by mouth.

The point is, to get the facts so you can make an educated decision on how to proceed. To this day I do not know the kind of cancer we were even dealing with. I can guess that it was an oral squamous cell carcinoma but I will never know for sure. There are new findings that in dogs and humans, that histone deacetylase inhibitors (HDAC) may be effective in slowing the growth and killing the tumor cells. It was not offered for Skeamer. My ignorance of the options, and my lack of understanding, are mistakes I will not make again.

There are several kinds of skin cancers: basal cell, squamous cell, mast cell, and fibrosarcoma, are the types typically seen in felines.

Lymphoma is the most commonly diagnosed feline cancer, accounting for about a third of all feline tumors. It infects the lymphoid tissue and can affect any organ, at any age. In the past lymphoma appeared to be associated with the feline leukemia virus or feline immunodeficiency virus. Since more cats are getting tested and vaccinated against FeLV and FIV, the average age of a cat with lymphoma is increasing, and is more often found in older cats than cats with those diseases.

Lymphoma is often divided into four groups: gastrointestinal (affecting the stomach and intestines), multicentric (lymph nodes, liver and spleen), mediastinal (chest cavity), and extranodal (other organs). Diagnosis is often done through a biopsy which will determine if the cancer is low-grade (small cell or lymphocytic) or high grade (large cell or lymphoblastic). Low grade, although more aggressive, typically is more likely to go into remission than high grade. Chemotherapy in some cases has been very successful in remission, from several months to a few years.

Mammary gland tumors are most common in older female cats that were not spayed before their first heat cycle, although male cats and altered cats can still be affected. Breast cancer is the third most common type of cancer seen in cats. Female cats spayed before six months of age are at a 91% reduced risk of mammary tumors.

If your cat is diagnosed with cancer you could make some good come out the situation and possibly help other cats. Ask your vet to record your cat's medical information with the Veterinary Cancer Registry at vetcancerregistry.com. The collected data and study may help with future treatment for other cats.

Seizures in cats are uncommon, apart from other underlying medical problems. It is possible for otherwise healthy cats to suffer from seizure disorders like epilepsy.

Without an underlying cause, the disorder is called idiopathic epilepsy. There may be a genetic link, but often the cause is unknown. Seizures usually begin between ages one and three. Daily medication can be given, but there is no cure.

PalaceDolls AbbyRose of RocknRagz (blue bicolor)

Arthritis or **osteoarthritis, OA,** can often be seen in older or overweight cats. As the life span increases, so do age-related problems, like arthritis. Arthritis is the loss of the cartridge, or cushioning between the joints and lubricating joint fluid that allows the bones to rub together.

We noticed with Skeamer that she seemed to hesitate to jump down from the sofa, no longer used the stairs, and had to readjust herself often, even though she napped on a very soft folded blanket. We preferred to go the natural route instead of using medication like anti-inflammatory or corticosteroids. We added chondroitin sulfate, glucosamine and omega oils to her diet. I think she probably suffered from arthritis for a while before the signs became obvious.

They now make joint supplements with several combined ingredients like chondroitin, glucosamine, omega fatty

Karen Wright of Kylador's Ragdoll with two kittens

Cognitive disorder or **senility** in cats with reduced brain function can exhibit signs similar to Alzheimer's disease (AD). Skeamer started showing some of these signs after she was about 14 or 15. We were not told about the drugs like *Novifit*, a form of SAMe, amitriptyline (*Elavil*) selegiline (*Deprenyl, or Anipryl*), to slow down its progression or ease the symptoms— maybe because she already had renal failure. You can also use some of the behavioral products like pheromone diffusers to calm your cat. We noticed first that she would have a dumbfounded look on her face and look around as if seeing her surroundings for the first time. She just looked confused as to where she was, or why she came into the room. It didn't help that we moved to a new home when she was 13 years old. We then started to hear our usually quiet cat howling during the night. Thyroid issues were suspected, and then ruled out as a cause.

acids, MSM, zinc, vitamin *C*, vitamin *E*, selenium, manganese, milk thistle, boswellia herb and red deer antler velvet to help with arthritis. OA is not curable, but adding a joint supplement under your veterinarian's approval may slow down the loss of cartridge and joint fluid. I will probably start Tyler and Trinity on a joint supplement when they are around seven regardless of whether or not they show symptoms.

Symptoms to watch for are inability to jump, altered gait, difficulty getting up, stiffness, limping, favoring a limb, licking or biting at a painful area, litter box avoidance, lethargy, decreased movement or appetite, vocalization, and irritable or reclusive behavior. Acupuncture, massage, heat, ultrasound treatment, and laser or physical therapy are thought to be beneficial.

Plain Old Age: The good news is that cats are now living long enough to be of age to get these old age aliments. The bad news is— they are not reversible.

Some of the decline we dismissed as old age, like her increased sleeping, lack of energy, blank stares, and decreased grooming. Some cats even stop using their litter box, forget to eat or drink, or do not recognize their family members. There are appetite stimulating drugs that may be needed because cats that go too long without eating can develop liver damage. This is a good time to have a postal or baby scale. It is hard, especially with long-haired cats to notice a weight change before a big change has already occurred.

Our scale stopped working near the end of Skeamer's life, but I could tell when I picked her up that she had lost weight. I think Skeamer always knew who we were; she never missed the litter box and never had a problem with wanting to eat. We considered adding additional litter boxes if she forgot where hers was, but she continued to faithfully use it. You may need to add a ramp to the litter box or change the type of box to a low sided box, add additional boxes or change the location to make it more easily accessible.

As Skeamer aged, she seemed to take less care in cleaning and grooming herself and her coat started to look neglected. We purchased new grooming brushes that she seemed to tolerate better than her old ones. She never liked to be groomed, but with age and her decreased ability to reach and clean everywhere, I think after we switched brushes she actually appreciated our help. When you are grooming or petting your elderly cat, it is even more important to feel for any changes in weight and feel for any lumps.

An elderly cat needs routine, and things left unchanged as much as possible. Don't move furniture around or leave things on the floor. If you can block-off parts of the house that your cat doesn't use often, it can keep your cat from going to unfamiliar areas by mistake and getting lost or confused. Keep everything accessible by limiting your elderly cat's access in your home by having all your cats needs, like food, water, litter boxes and sleeping space, on one floor so it will not be required to use the stairs, that may be painful.

Your elderly or senior cat needs you to notice slight changes in behavior. Watch for eating or litter box changes, and take notice of the little things, like lack of using the stairs or jumping that may signal arthritis. An elderly cat's digestive system becomes less efficient and they may need food supplements or a probiotic added to help it manage the good bacteria balance. You should talk to your vet about your cats dietary needs at this point in their life, and consider slowly changing over to a food specific to your elderly cat's needs. Discuss dietary supplements after having blood work done. Dental care at this age is extremely important. You should also increase your vet visits to twice a year.

Your elderly cat will likely prefer a soft bed and warm places to sleep. You can purchase heated beds and heated window perches. There is pain management you can discuss with your vet if you feel like your cat is in pain, including medication or alternative therapy, or a combination of the two, to make sure your cat's last years are as comfortable as possible. We used makeshift stools and ottomans to make steps so our old girl could get to her favorite napping spots. They make pet steps you can purchase so that your cat can still enjoy getting to their favorite napping spot. Give plenty of love, interaction and easy play time to encourage stretching and mental function. This is the time for your elderly cat to be as comfortable, mentally and physically as you can make it, avoiding stress, changes, or new pets.

I bought three books trying to learn what to expect or watch for with my elderly cat that I would recommend. They are listed in the "Resources and Reference" section.

Karen Wright of Kylador's Leif and Autumn

Sandy Baker's Ember (Bengal), Sasha (Siamese), Rocky and Pippin (Ragdolls)

Saying Goodbye

Skeamer at five weeks old, and age 12 or 13

Tyler and Trinity two months old,
then each birthday first through fourth

My pets are my children. I celebrate new arrivals, adoption anniversaries, birthdays, and cherish the years and memories. I also mourn a death like losing a part of my family. It is hard for me to understand those who think of pets as "just animals."

If your pet is ill before it passes, you may grieve before you actually lose your pet. Some veterinarians now offer hospice care for pets. This brings up another point. Do you have written plans, like a will, or pet trust stating what is to happen if your cat outlives you or you are unable to care for it? It is a good idea to have instructions in writing, in case you are unable to care for your cat due to injury, illness, or death. There are several options, but when the unexpected or inevitable happens, you owe it to your pets to have their future taken care of. You can leave specific instructions in your will; let a family member or an appointed custodian know what your wishes are and who you would like to take care of your cats. If you do not have someone in mind, you could specify a specific cat rescue organization, cat sanctuary, or lifetime care facility.

I never had to make the decision to euthanize a pet before Skeamer, and I did not know what to expect. It was nothing like I had imagined. Everyone told me that I would know when it was time. I knew on Friday night. I cried and I prayed that she would pass peacefully in her sleep, but that was not to be. At some level, I was in denial. I had planned to have the vet come to our home when it was time because Skeamer stressed so much when I took her to the clinic. I was holding on to a thread of hope that a tooth was causing her pain.

My Tyler and Trinity

Lynn Freeman's Dinky (seal bicolor)
and Nolte (blue bicolor)

Constance McCarthy's Nicodemus (seal
colorpoint) and Ezekiel (seal point mitted)

Patricia Besaw's Bellapalazzo Sir Bentley and
Bellapalazzo Maximillion (both BEW, blue-eyed white)

Karen Wright of Kylador's Ragdolls cuddling

Linda Dicmanis' Schniffley (seal colorpoint)
and Bingo (blue colorpoint)

The cancer had broken her jaw the night before, and it was time. It was hard not to be selfish and want to keep her with us longer. All she had left was eating, sleeping, and being loved, but when she could not get comfortable, couldn't eat, and was in obvious pain— we knew it was best for her, to let her go. My cousin Shaylene put it best, "We did it for her— not to her."

My husband made a nice cedar box that we engraved with her name and an outline drawing of her face. I drew a life-size silhouette of her and had it made out of metal to mark her grave. At first I had a hard time seeing it outside, knowing she had been an indoor cat all her life. Now, when I look outside and see her silhouette, it brings back memories of her sitting just like that.

I saved a lock of Skeamer's fur that I placed in a frame with her picture. I have heard of people doing a casting of a paw print to put in a shadow box. You can even have a a print casting made in to jewelry or an ornament. Just remember that there is no right or wrong way to grieve. You are not going to feel the exact same way as someone else. Grief is as individual as each relationship and each cat. For me, I found making a memory book filled with pictures, short stories, nicknames and

traits about Skeamer helped. I also found comfort in chatting online with other cat lovers. There are many resources in the back of the book you may find helpful in coping with loss.

Your other pets may mourn or show signs of depression. They too can experience grief, and handle the healing process differently. There are flower essences that help some cats, like honeysuckle, gentian, walnut, red chestnut, chicory, heather, gorse or bleeding heart.

When we lost Skeamer after so long together, I said I did not want another pet. It was just too hard to let go. I so wished that pets lived longer. For weeks afterward, I kept "seeing" her in her favorite spots, or coming around a corner in the house.

Our house began to feel empty without a furbaby running around and I knew that getting another cat or two, was what I needed to do. I added my name to a Ragdoll rescue group in late May, and I brought home my two Ragdoll wannabes the first week of June. I never thought I would find exactly what I was looking for so fast. The good part is that watching them play, and learning their personalities cannot help but make me smile.

Lynn Freeman's Dinky (seal bicolor)
and Nolte (blue bicolor)

*W*hen you are ready, you can rest assured knowing there is a big blue-eyed floppy cat just waiting to snuggle, purr and flop its way right in to you heart.

Not to replace, but to start again, learning another cat's quirks, and traits, making new memories.

Whether it's laughing at a kitten's silly antics or connecting with an older cat's simple head-tilt, love and time, both heal. Before you know it, they will have you wrapped around their furry paws, enriching both human and feline lives.

Karen Wright of Kylador's seal point mitted kitten

Marsha Harris' Tessie (seal point mitted)

Alissa Pendorf's Raina is a blue lynx bicolor from breeder *Jazzmania*. Back cover bottom photo is Alissa's Raina doing the Ragdoll flop.

Angela Kostelansky of *Three Rivers Ragdolls* ThreeRiversRagdolls.com "A small home cattery near Pittsburgh PA. We breed minks as well as traditional colors and patterns."

Anthony Gonzales of *Beauty Purrs Cattery,* breeding Persians.

Barbara Müller-Walter's Maxwell Smart, was a black silver classic tabby Maine Coon.

Caroline Parris' seal colorpoint wannabe, Angel.

Cindy Forst's Lili, is an SPCA rescue who is a blue colorpoint.

Constance McCarthy's Nicodemus was a seal colorpoint. Ezekiel, is a seal point mitted. Nicodemus was Ezekiel's Uncle from *Sugar Plum Ragdolls* in Auburn California.

Debbie Le-Strange of *Guys n Dolls.* "Registered breeder in Queensland, Australia breeding home raised beautiful, healthy Ragdolls." GuysnDollsRagdolls.com

Debra F. Payne of *Blumoon O' Kentucky* Cattery breeding Siamese and American Wirehairs. BluMoonSiamese.com

Eve Kurpiers' Snuggler is a chocolate torbie bicolor and Nuzzler, a blue bicolor.

Gail Vettel of *Angel Kissed Ragdolls* "The Ragdoll truly is a remarkable breed."

Gloie Wall's Benji is a flame point mitted lynx and Katie, a seal colorpoint and Jamie the Sheltie.

Jenny Moylan's Shiloh, is a flame bicolor. Her

dog Indy along with a non-Ragdoll kitten are also featured.

Karen Wilkinson's four Ragdolls are Gizmo a cream bicolor, Fred also a cream bicolor, Merlin who is a seal point mitted and Myst a blue colorpoint. They are from Julie Emery of *Yremer Ragdolls*. Merlin and Myst are litter brothers, as are Gizmo and Fred.

Karen Wright of *Kylador* "Small cattery breeding traditional Ragdolls. Our cats are registered with TICA. Kittens are well socialized, healthy and loving. Before they leave they are always spayed/neutered, micro-chipped and have received their first two vaccinations. Three year health guarantee and daily videos while you are waiting for your kitten. Raised underfoot with retrievers that we also breed." Back cover, top photo is Kylador's Basil, a blue bicolor. Kylador.com

Kevin Wright's Spencer. No papers but was told he was a purebred.

Krista Tulle's Zeus is a blue bicolor from *Kylador Ragdolls*. Chance the lab is pictured also.

Kristi Pemberton of *Big City Dolls Ragdoll* Cattery located in Cincinnati, Ohio. "We offer traditional Ragdolls as well as minks, sepias and solids. We focus on breeding for health and temperament thus producing beautiful healthy kittens with wonderful personalities." BigCityDolls.com

Laurie Nicholson of *Rock n Ragz* RocknRagz.com

Linda Dicmanis' Schniffley, a seal colorpoint and Bingo, who is a blue colorpoint are both from *Ragd'vine Ragdolls*.

Lynn Freeman's Nolte is a blue bicolor and Dinky was a seal bicolor.

Lynn Jasper's Supurrags Princess Isabella, "Bella" is a seal point mitted.

Macair Skelton-Angeles' RockstarDolls Sir Augustine. "Auggie" is a blue A-typical bicolor.

Marsha Harris' Quincy is a male flame bicolor and Tessie, the female seal point mitted that is on the front cover. Both cats are from *Fur Real Ragdolls* and are half brother and sister.

Mary Becker's Tedrick "Teddy" is a seal lynx mitted with a mismark hourglass on his face, from *Pams Dollhouse Ragdoll* Cattery and Toulouse "Touie" is a blue point mitted with a small blaze from *Gwennor Ragdolls*.

Mary Susan McAuliff of *Windy-Gables Ragdolls* in Richmond, VA "Breeding traditional and mink Ragdolls since 2006." Windy-Gables.com

Melissa Firestone of *RockstarDolls Ragdolls* in Virginia. RockstarRagdolls.com

Mrs. Mary Ewen of *DrouinDolls*.

Nancy East's O'Malley is a chocolate lynx mitted, Reilly a blue cream mitted, and Murphey a flame colorpoint who is "gone buy not forgotten 10/19/02-07/14/03." All cats from *Abadabadolls*. Shea the German Shepherd is pictured also.

Photographer Nyree Glapp's Meddle, a black silver tabby blotched Maine Coon.

Patricia Besaw's Bellapalazzo Sir Bentley and Bellapalazzo Maximillion are both blue-eyed white Ragdolls, as registered in TICA.

Pia Venbrant of *Hvenhildas* in Sweden "has been breeding since 1991, started with Ragdolls in 1997."

Rovena E. Parmley of *Tuftytoes Ragdoll Cats*, "Original breeder cats came from Ann Baker and IRCA. Breeding large, loving, and "floppy" Ragdolls in point and non-pointed (solid) colors since 1982." Member of RI, RFCI, TICA, and TICA Keestone Katz Cat Club.

Sandy Baker's Rocky is from *Cathedral Ragdolls* and is a seal lynx mitted. Pippin is a seal mitted with blaze. Nicky the Dalmatian, Holly the Hungarian Vizsla and Duncan a Quaker parrot are also featured.

Shalane Doucette of *Palace Cats* Ragdolls and Sphynx in Florida. Back cover middle photo is PalaceCats Armani, a seal mitted kitten.

Shirley Stubrich's Mick, is a seal bicolor, Marley is a blue bicolor, both are from *Kylador*. Rajah is a blue colorpoint.

Sonja Phillips' Cody Blue is a blue colorpoint and Tucker Bee a, seal point mitted. Brody was a seal bicolor who died at 13 months after being exposed and contracting FIP. Brothers Cody and Tucker are from *Kelbrier* and are leap year babies.

Stephanie Green's Kasseldolls Identity Crisis "Janet" is a blue bicolor.

Susan Thompson's Dollheaven Tinkerbell is a blue torbie point mitted and Dollheaven Tallulah a blue bicolor.

Suzanne Leonhard of *Hollywood Rags* HollywoodRagdolls.com

Tara Rerrie's Dixter, a red mackerel tabby RagaMuffin.

Wain Pearce historian and copyright holder of the early Ragdoll / Baker photos, for the Ragdoll Fanciers Club International (RFCI) rfci.org/history/pictorial-history/index.php

Resources and References

AACE American Association of Cat Enthusiast (USA) aaceinc.org

ACF Australian Cat Federations acf.asn.au

ACFA American Cat Fanciers Association (USA) acfacat.com

Australian National Cat Inc formerly WNCA (Australia) ancats.com.au

Capital Cats Inc (Australia) cci.asn.au

CAT Cat Association of Tasmania (Australia) catinc.org.au

CATZ Inc (New Zealand) catzinc.org

CAV The Cat Authority of Victoria Inc (Australia)

CCA Canadian Cat Association, AFC Association Féline Canadienne cca-afc.com/en

CCCA Coordinating Cat Council of Australia ccofa.asn.au

CCCT Cat Control Council of Tasmania Inc (Australia) ccctas.com

CCEU Cat club Europe catclub-europe.com/index.php?lang=english

CFA Cat Fanciers Association (USA) cfa.org

CFCCQ Council of Federated Cat Clubs of Queensland Inc (Australia) cfccq.org

CFF Cat Fanciers Federation (USA) cffinc.org

CFSA Cat Federation of Southern Africa cfsa.co.za

COAWA Cat Owners Association of Western Australia coawa.com

EGCA European Group Cat Association int-egca.de

FANSW Feline Association of New South Wales Inc (Australia) tfansw.com.au

FASA Feline Association of South Australia felineassociationsa.com

FB Felis Britannica (UK) felisbritannica.co.uk

FCCQ Feline Control Council of Queensland Inc (Australia) fccqinc.org.au

FCCV Feline Control Council of Victoria Inc (Australia) hotkey.net.au/~fccvic/fccv2a.htm

FCCWA Feline Control council of Western Australia felinecontrolcouncilofwesternaustralia.com.au

Felis Britiannica (Britain) *formerly CA Cat Association* felisbritannica.co.uk

FFFE Fédération Féline Française (France) fifeweb.org

FIAF Federazione Italiana Associazioni Feline (Italy) fiafonline.it

FiFe Fédération Internationale Féline fifeweb.org

GCCF Governing Council of the Cat Fancy (UK) gccfcats.org

GCCFSA Governing Council of the Cat Fancy of South Australia users.chariot.net.au/~gccfsa

GCCFV Governing Council of the Cat Fancy Victoria (Australia) cats.org.au

IFA International Feline Association mfa-ifa.ru

NRR Norwegian pedigree Clubs Riksförbund (Norway) nrr.no

NSWCFA New South Wales Cat Fanciers Association (Australia) *formerly RASCC* nswcfa.asn.au/NSW%20CFA.htm

NZCF New Zealand Cat Fancy nzcatfancy.gen.nz

QFA Queensland Feline Association Inc (Australia) qfeline.com

QICC Queensland Independent Cat Council Inc (Australia) qicc.org.au

RAG Ragdolls of America Group ragdollscfa.org

REFR Rare and Exotic Feline Registry rareandexoticfelinereg.homestead.com

RFC Ragdoll Fanciers Club ragdollfanciersclub.org

RFCI Ragdoll Fanciers Club International rfci.org

SACC Southern Africa Cat Council tsacc.org.za

TICA The International Cat Association tica.org

UFO United Feline organization (USA) unitedfelineorganization.net

WCC World Cat Congress worldcatcongress.org

WCF World Cat Federation wcf-online.de

Show Schedules

acfacat.com/show_schedule.htm
cfa.org/exhibitors/show-schedule.html
ticamembers.org/calendar

Books

A Ragdoll Kitten Care Guide: Bringing Your Ragdoll Kitten Home book by Jenny Dean of floppycats.com

Guide to Owning a Ragdoll Cat by Gary A. Strobel and Susan A.Nelson

Ragdoll Cat by Denise Jones

Ragdoll Cats by Karen Leigh Davis

The Definitive Guide to Ragdolls, published by Ragdoll World UK (out of print) by Lorna Wallace, Robin Pickering and David Polland

Think Like a Cat by Pam Johnson-Bennett

Aging Cat by Amy D. Shojai

The Older Cat by Dan Poynter

Your Older Cat by Susan Easterly

Magazines and Newsletter

All About Cats magazine
Cat Fancy magazine
Cat Talk Almanac magazine
Cat World International magazine
Catnip newsletter
Cats & Kittens magazine
Cats magazine
Cats USA magazine
Catwatch newsletter
Catworld magazine
I love Cats magazine
TICA Trend bimonthly publication
Your Cat (UK) magazine

RagaMuffin

CFA RagaMuffin
cfa.org/Client/breedRagaMuffin.aspx

CFA RagaMuffin standard cfa.org/documents/breeds/standards/ragamuffin.pdf

RagaMuffin Associated Group ragamuffingroup.com

Ragdoll Specific

ACF Australian Cat Federation Ragdoll breed standard acfacat.com/ragdoll_standard.htm

CFA Ragdoll breed profile and standard
cfa.org/Client/breedRagdoll.aspx
cfa.org/documents/breeds/standards/ragdoll.pdf

International Ragdoll Congress
internationalragdollcongress.org

Pawpeds Ragdoll database
pawpeds.com/db/?p=rag&date=iso

Purebred Cat Rescue Ragdoll
purebredcatbreedrescue.org/ragdoll.htm

Ragdoll Breed Club ragdollbreedclub.org

Ragdoll Fanciers Club International (RFCI) rfci.org

Ragdoll Fanciers Club (RFC) ragdollfanciersclub.org

Ragdoll Fanciers Worldwide (RFW) rfwclub.org

Ragdoll Historical Society ragdollhistoricalsociety.com

Ragdoll International ragdollinternational.org

Ragdoll Research ragdollresearch.org

Ragdoll World online ragdollworldonline.com

Ragdolls of America Group (RAG) ragdollscfa.org

The British Ragdoll Cat Club tbrcc.co.uk

The Ragdoll Connection Network ragdoll-cats.com

TICA Ragdoll and Ragdoll breed standard
tica.org/public/breeds/rd/intro.php
tica.org/members/publications/standards/rd.pdf

Ragdoll Yahoo! Groups

pets.groups.yahoo.com/group/floppycats
pets.groups.yahoo.com/group/Ragdoll-Cat
pets.groups.yahoo.com/group/ragdolllovers
pets.groups.yahoo.com/group/ragdolls
pets.groups.yahoo.com/group/RagdollsRock
pets.groups.yahoo.com/group/theBestofRagdolls

Certified Animal Behavior Consultant CABC

American College of Veterinary Behaviorist
veterinarybehaviorists.org

Animal Behavior Society (ABS)
animalbehaviorsociety.org

International Association of Animal Behavior
Consultants iaabc.org

Abused, Lost, Rescue, Rehome, Retired

Adoptapet adoptapet.com/cat-adoption

American Humane Association Americanhumane.org/animals

Animal Shelter Animalshelter.org

Animals and Society Institute animalsandsociety.org/resources/index.php?pid=23&tpid=7

ASPCA ASPCA.org/Fight-Animal-Cruelty.aspx

CFA Breed Rescue Program and retired Ragdolls
cfabreedersassist-rescue.org/rescue.html
ragdollscfa.org/availableretirees.php

Find Toto FindToto.com

FloppyCats.com
blog.floppycats.com/blog/ragdoll-rehoming

Lost Pet USA (lost or found) lostpetusa.net

Merlins Hope on Facebook
facebook.com/merlinshope.ragdollrescue

No Paws Left Behind (foreclosure)
NoPawsLeftBehind.org/paws/Home/Main.aspx

Petfinder (lost or found) petfinder.com/local.html

Purebred Cat Breed Rescue
purebredcatbreedrescue.org/ragdoll.htm

Purebred Plus Cat Rescue
purebredsplus.org/available/rag_bir.html

Rescue Me rescueme.org

RFW club rfwclub.org/ragdolladult.htm

Ragdolls International
ragdollinternational.org/brdrsretired.shtml#retired

Ragdoll Rescue freewebs.com/ragdollrescue
the place that posted my two cats as Ragdoll wannabe's

Ragdoll Rescue NW ragdollrescue.com

Ragdoll Rescue USA ragdollrescueusa.webs.com

SpotLite SpotLight GPS Spotlightgps.com

Yahoo! Group Ragdoll Rescue USA Adopters pets.groups.yahoo.com/group/ragdollrescueusaadopters

Yahoo! Group Ragdoll Rescue USA
pets.groups.yahoo.com/group/RagdollRescueUSA

Food

AAFCO Association Of American Feed Control Officials, Inc. aafco.org

FDA Cat Food Recalls accessdata.fda.gov/scripts/newpetfoodrecalls/#Cat

Food and Drug Administration FDA.gov

Free Kibble -feed hungry pets by visiting clickingfreekibblekat.com

Petsumer Report PetsumerReport.com

The Environmental Working Group pet health ewg.org/pethealth

Truth About Pet Food TruthAboutPetFood.com

Medical and Health

2nd Chance 4 Pets lifetime care for your pets 2ndchance4pets.org

Alley Cat Allies alleycat.org

American Animal Hospital Association aahanet.org

American Association of Feline Practitioners (find a specialist) catvets.com

American Veterinary Medical Association avma.org

Asthma, Feline Asthma felineasthma.org

Cat Health cathealth.com

Companion Animal Parasite Council CAPC petsandparasites.org/cat-owners

Cornell University College of Veterinary Medicine feline health www.vet/cornell.edu/FHC

Cornell University College of Veterinary Medicine Partners in health partnersah.vet.cornell.edu/pet/cats

Delta Society now Pet Partners petpartners.org

Drs. Foster and Smith, Overweight Cat? peteducation.com/article.cfm?c=1+2230&aid=660

Feline Advisory Bureau fabcats.org

HCM in Ragdolls Feline Advisory Bureau (FAB) fabcats.org/hcm

Herpes, Feline Herpes Yahoo! Group pets.groups.yahoo.com/group/felineherpes

Humane Society HumaneSociety.org/animals/cats

Insurance, Pet Insurance Review, compare rates and benefits petinsurancereview.com/cat.asp

Just answer justanswer.com/cat-health

Kitten Care KittenCare.com

Know Your Cat KnowYourCat.info

Morris Animal Foundation MorrisAnimalFoundation.org

My Veterinarian (find a vet in your area) myveterinarian.com/avma/vclPublic

NC State University College of Veterinary medicine (genetics lab) cvm.ncsu.edu

Pet Alert PetAlertDecal.com/decal_info.htm

Spay USA spayusa.org

The Safety Reporting Portal https://www.safetyreporting.hhs.gov/fpsr

UPENN research involving animals upenn.edu/research/rcr/animals.htm

Veterinary Oral Health Council vohc.org

Vetinfo VetInfo.com/category/cats

WebMd for cats pets.webmd.com/cats

Winn Feline Foundation WinnFelineHealth.org

Alternative, Herbal, Holistic and Homeopathy

American Botanical Council herbalgram.org

American Holistic Veterinary Medical Association ahvma.org

Herb Research at herbs.org

Herbal medicine National Animal Supplement council nasc.cc

Holistic Cat Flower Essences/remedies holisticat.com/fes.html

Holistic Vet list holisticvetlist.com

Holistic veterinary aava.org

Holistic veterinary ivas.org

National Animal Supplement Council nasc.cc

The Academy of Veterinary Homeopathy theavh.org

The American Academy of Veterinary Acupuncture aava.org

The International Veterinary Acupuncture Society ivas.org

Tractional Chinese Veterinary Medicine TCVM search.tcvm.com/vetFinding.asp?qtype=zip

Veterinary Botanical Medical vbma.org

Cancer

ACF Animal Cancer Foundation acfoundation.org

Cancer, VCS Veterinary Cancer Society vetcancersociety.org

Cancer, Vet Cancer Registry vetcancerregistry.com

CRF, Chronic Renal Failure

Feline CRF Information center felinecrf.com

Feline CRF on Yahoo! pets.groups.yahoo.com/group/felineCRF

Feline CRF Support on Yahoo! pets.groups.yahoo.com/group/feline-crf-support

Diabetes

Defeat Diabetes defeatdiabetes.org/about_diabetes/text.asp?id=PetDiabetes_CatsDogs

Feline Diabetes felinediabetes.com

My Cat has Diabetes mycathasdiabetes.com

Diabetes, Pet Diabetes petdiabetes.com

DNA

Cat Genes catgenes.org and catdnatest.org

UC Davis Veterinary Medicine feline test
vgl.ucdavis.edu/services/cat
Feline coat color test symbols
vgl.ucdavis.edu/services/coatcolorcat.php
Feline genetics laboratory
vetmed.ucdavis.edu/Catgenetics
Feline ancestry
vgl.ucdavis.edu/services/cat/ancestry

Washington State University Veterinary Genetics Laboratory http://www.ncstatevets.org/genetics/

Heartworm

Know Heartworms knowheartworms.org

The American Heartworm Society heartwormsociety.org

Poisoning

ASPCA list of toxic plants aspca.org/pet-care/poison-control/plants/?plant_toxicity=toxic-to-cats

ASPCA Poison hotline, call 1-888-426-4435 or visit aspca.org/pet-care/poison-control

ASPCA Poison Control list aspca.org/pet-care/ask-the-expert/ask-the-expert-poison-control

AVMA First Aid Tips for Pet Owners avma.org/firstaid

Pet Poison Helpline 1-800-213-6680 or visit petpoisonhelpline.com

Vaccines or Vaccinations

CFA's vaccination guidelines cfa.org/client/healthvaccinationguidelines.aspx

Critter Advocacy critteradvocacy.org

Vaccines or Vaccinations continued

VAFSTF Vaccine-Associated Feline Sarcoma Task Force avma.org/vafstf

Hospice, Pet Loss, Grief, and Memorials

Animal Love and Loss Network (ALLn) alln.org/aboutus.cfm

Argus Institute csuvth.colostate.edu/diagnostic_and_support/argus

ASPCA pet loss at 1-877-474-3310 aspca.org/pet-care/pet-loss 1-877-GRIEF-10

Association for Pet Loss Bereavement aplb.org

C.A.R.E pet loss helpline (877) 394-CARE (2273) vetmed.illinois.edu/CARE

Cornell University College of Veterinary Medicine 607-253-3932 vet.cornell.edu/org/petloss

Delta Society now Pet Partners petpartners.org petpartners.org/Page.aspx?pid=307

Michigan State College of Veterinary medicine cvm.msu.edu/alumni-friends/information-for-animal-owners/pet-loss-support

Ontario Veterinary College 519-824-4120 ext 53694 ovc.uoguelph.ca/petloss

Pet Loss Help petlosshelp.org

The International Association of Animal Hospice and Palliative Care iaahpc.org

The Ohio State University Veterinary Medical Center vet.osu.edu/vmc/honoring-bond-pet-owner-support

Tufts University tufts.edu/vet/petloss

University of California at Davis School of Veterinary Medicine vetmed.ucdavis.edu/ccab/petloss.html

University of Illinois College of Veterinary Medicine 877-394-CARE cvm.uiuc.edu/CARE

Washington State University Pet loss support 1-(866) 266-8635 vetmed.wsu.edu/PLHL

Travel

Care.com care.com/pets

Happy Tails Travel happytailstravel.com

National Association of Professional Pet Sitters (NAPPS) petsitters.org

Pet Airways petairways.com

Pet Flight petflight.com

Pet Sitter petsitter.com

Pet Sitters International petsit.com

The Independent Pet and Animal Transportation Association International Inc ipata.com

Trip with Pets tripwithpets.com

About the Author

KimberlyMaxwell.com
facebook.com/KimberlyHMaxwell
gplus.to/KimberlyMaxwell
twitter.com/#!/KHMaxwell

Kim has been an animal lover since childhood, bringing home animals, often injured animals, or pleading to keep a stray. She had all sorts of animals, but was never allowed to have a cat.

Shortly after she married, her cousin called, who is now a veterinarian, and told her about available kittens. She jumped at the chance and brought home a little fluff ball they named Skeamer. Her husband jokes that he missed that part in their wedding vows which stated they just had to have pets.

She worked in furniture sales and interior design for twenty years, and was self-employed for the last fifteen of those years. She felt like she needed to move on and try something different. She considered pet-sitting or working with a veterinarian, but her husband, knowing how much she liked animals, especially those in need, did not think much of those ideas.

She closed her business without knowing what would follow. A few months later she had a desire to make a coffee table photo book, but when she started on that, the idea evolved in to a full fledged detailed book about Ragdoll cats.

In addition to her love of cats, especially Ragdolls, she enjoys spending time with her family and friends, photography, and all aspects of design. She also has a heart for Jesus.

She lives in the Western North Carolina mountains with her husband of over twenty years, and their two cats, Tyler and Trinity that she found through an online Ragdoll rescue website.

Legal & General

Registration.

email (jicelive.co.uk)

Security questions:

① Childhood Pet — 'Tiddles'

② "Ford Popular"

③ Film — "The Firm"

Q4 User ID:

Vortex100

Password:

~~Meditation55~~

Meditation#55

Lightning Source UK Ltd.
Milton Keynes UK
UKHW05f2004290418
321837UK00004BA/67/P